GLOW UP
YOUR GRADES

The ULTIMATE GUIDE to TRANSFORMING your
ENGLISH GCSE

with *Mehreen Baig*

plus video support

CONTENTS

A Note from Mehreen

Dear Students,

I know you want to get started on your revision, but I just wanted to write you a quick note first.

GCSEs can be a stressful time, and it's totally normal to feel nervous. But you will be absolutely fine, because I have put EVERYTHING I know into this revision guide and, by the end of it, you will feel SO much more confident. Just trust the process.

I decided to create 'Glow Up Your Grades' because I truly believe that every child deserves the chance to do well in their education and to build a good future for themselves. The time and effort you put in now will, one day, give you the chance to create a better life for yourself and those around you.

You've already done the hardest part! You have bought this revision guide and are reading the first page. I am SO proud of you. Now leave the rest to me! Work through this guide slowly and, together, we will conquer all your fears. There are links to some of my videos for some extra practice too – so by the time you walk into that exam hall, you'll basically be Shakespeare.

I am so excited for you. Work hard and make yourself proud. You've got this.

Mehreen

xxx

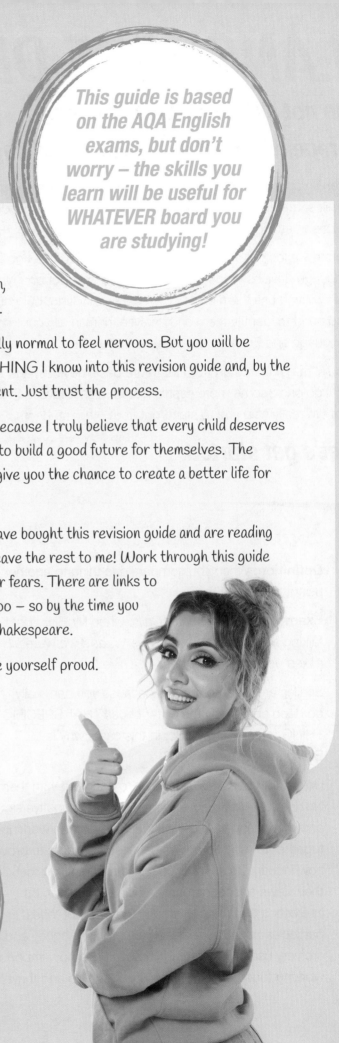

LANGUAGE DEVICES

For more on this, see my video:

Do not skip over these pages.
I repeat, do not skip over these pages.

Even if you think you already know your literary terminology (similes, metaphors, etc.), keep reading. I promise you, you will learn something new.

Before we look at any exam questions, you NEED to know your language devices inside out. They are super important. Not only will you use them in your own creative writing, but you will also need to identify them and analyse them in all your English Language and English Literature exams!

So… I'm going to start from the more basic devices, and then we'll go on to some more sophisticated, higher-level terminology that will really help you to stand out from other students.

Let's get started.

Simile

Definition: When you compare one thing to another using 'like' or 'as'.

Example: In *An Inspector Calls*, when Mr Birling is talking about socialism, he says '… *as if we were all mixed up together like bees in a hive.*'

Similes are great to analyse because you can really go deep about why the writer chose THAT SPECIFIC THING to compare to. So, in this case, why is Mr Birling talking about bees?

Do you like bees? Do you want to hang out with them? No. Hence, Mr Birling is using a typically negative simile and comparing the socialist idea of everyone working together to *'bees in a hive'* because he wants to prove how irritating that would be, and he is implying that their views are dangerous to society. However, it's interesting that Priestley chose the simile of *'bees'* in particular, because bees actually produce honey and are very useful… but Mr Birling can't see how important working together is for humanity to survive and thrive!

TOP TIP!

Students often spell SIMILE incorrectly, and slide in an extra I after the L. Be careful that you spell it right! It's simiLE – not simiLIE.

Metaphor

Definition: When you compare two things WITHOUT using 'like' or 'as'. It's a bit like when your teacher tells you that you're a star – you're not really a star. It's a metaphor.

Example: In *An Inspector Calls*, Sheila says, *'You mustn't try to build up a wall between us and that girl… the Inspector will just break it down.'*

No one is literally building a wall. It's a metaphor. Sheila is suggesting that her family has created an impenetrable divide between themselves and Eva Smith – symbolic of the class divide between the rich and the poor in Edwardian society.

Hyperbole

Definition: Exaggeration. I use hyperbole all the time. I always say things like, 'This is the WORST DAY OF MY LIFE'… when it probably isn't. I'm exaggerating. I'm using hyperbole. I'm being hyperbolic.

Example: In *A Christmas Carol*, Dickens describes how the *'mighty blaze'* next to the Ghost of Christmas Present *'went roaring up the chimney'*. The hyperbolic description of the heat here juxtaposes the earlier description of Scrooge's *'feeble fire'*.

TOP TIP!

If you want to be really sophisticated in your essay, you can combine hyperbole with simile or metaphor. You can say, 'The writer's use of this hyperbolic metaphor shows…', which just means an exaggerated metaphor.

Personification

Definition: When you give human qualities to something that's not human. Like *'the trees waved at me.'* Trees can't wave – humans wave. It's personification. (Trees waving is a bit cliché so you don't want to use it in your creative writing… but you get what I mean.)

Example: In the poem 'Exposure', Owen personifies the winter and says, *'the merciless iced east winds that knive us'* to make the weather almost seem more deadly than the war itself.

Alliteration

Definition: When two or more words in a sentence start with the same letter or sound.

Example: In the poem 'Ozymandias', it says, *'the lone and level sands stretch far away'*, which creates an echoing effect and conveys how isolated and empty the desert is, showing his empire did not last.

TOP TIP!

Alliteration doesn't have to be EVERY SINGLE word in the sentence, and the words don't have to be right next to each other. If you see a sentence where two or more words that are close to each other start with the same letter or sound, it's still alliteration.

NOW – let's get posh.

If you're feeling fancy and want to impress your examiner, alliteration can branch off into different strands.

Plosive alliteration

Definition: Alliteration of a hard sound. (I remember it because it kind of sounds like EXPLOSIVE.) So, it's alliteration of letters like P, B, D or T.

Example: In 'The Charge of the Light Brigade', it says, *'Theirs but to do and die'*, and the strong sound created through the plosive alliteration emphasises the soldiers' courage.

Let's go deeper. We can separate all the plosive sounds into even more specific types of alliteration.

Dental plosive alliteration

Definition: Alliteration of a hard sound where the teeth meet… so D or T.

Example: In the poem 'Extract from *The Prelude*', the speaker says, *'With trembling oars I turned'*, and the dental plosive alliteration here creates a stuttering effect, highlighting his fear.

Bilabial plosive alliteration

Definition: Alliteration of a hard sound where your two lips touch. So that would be the letters B or P.

Example: In the poem 'Porphyria's Lover', it says *'…Blushed bright beneath my burning kiss'*, and the harsh sound mirrors the speaker's violence and possessive attitude.

Guttural alliteration

Definition: Alliteration of any sound from the back of your throat, G/C/K.

Example: In the poem 'When We Two Parted', Byron writes, *'Pale grew thy cheek and **c**old,/ **C**older thy **k**iss'*, and the choking sound created through the guttural alliteration mirrors the speaker's grief as he is unable to articulate his pain to his lover.

Sibilance

Definition: The sounds 'S', 'SH' or 'Z'. To be honest, I don't know why alliteration of these sounds has its own special word. I think it's because sibilance can have so many different effects – like it can be soothing and peaceful… sinister and snaky… secretive and quiet… There are so many things you can say about it.

Example: In the poem, 'My Last Duchess', it says that *'all **s**miles **s**topped together'*, and the sibilance shows how sinister the duke's actions were, whereas in 'Winter Swans', the speaker says, *'I noticed our hand**s**, that had, **s**omehow,/ **s**wum the di**s**tan**c**e between u**s**'*, and the soft, gentle sibilance here reinforces that the couple has finally found peace after their conflict.

Fricative alliteration

Definition: Alliteration of F or PH or V.

Example: In the opening of *Macbeth*, fricative alliteration is used when the witches say, *'**F**air is **f**oul, and **f**oul is **f**air:/ Hover through the **f**og and **f**ilthy air'*, and this creates a spitting sound, as if they are drooling with excitement at the thought of the chaos they are about to cause.

RIGHT, that's enough alliteration. Or should I say… ample alliteration. Get it? Anyway, let's move on.

Rule of three

Definition: When you say something in three different ways for emphasis. Your teacher might call it a power of three, tricolon, triplet... but it all means the same thing.

Example: In the opening of *Romeo and Juliet*, Tybalt says, *'... As I hate hell, all Montagues, and thee.'* Here, the rule of three emphasises Tybalt's rage and aggression, and perhaps symbolises how long this anger has been festering inside him.

List

Definition: When you give more than three examples of something in a sentence.

Example: In the poem 'Mother, any distance', the speaker says, *'You come to help me measure windows, pelmets, doors,/ the acres of the walls, the prairies of the floors.'* The list could be emblematic of the fact that the speaker feels overwhelmed and is justifying why he isn't quite ready to let his mum go yet.

Asyndetic list

Definition: A list that only uses commas, without any conjunctions (e.g. doesn't say AND).

Example: In the opening description of Scrooge in *A Christmas Carol,* Dickens introduces him as *'a squeezing, wrenching, grasping, scraping, clutching, covetous old sinner...'.* The asyndetic list portrays how Scrooge's vices are never-ending.

Repetition

Definition: When you say the same thing more than once.

Example: In the poem 'The Charge of the Light Brigade', Tennyson repeats *'Half a league, half a league,/ Half a league…'*, which creates a dramatic rhythm and enhances the feeling of galloping horses.

TOP TIP!

This is another word that students spell incorrectly all the time. Be careful – it's repEtition. Not replEtition.

Onomatopoeia

Definition: When a word imitates a sound, like CRASH or BANG.

Example: In *The Strange Case of Dr Jekyll and Mr Hyde*, when Poole and Utterson break down the door of Jekyll's laboratory, the narrator describes the sound as, *'a dismal **screech**, as of mere animal terror, **rang** from the cabinet'*.

The onomatopoeia in *'screech'* and *'rang'* evokes the reader's senses and shows that, as Hyde, Jekyll's pain is so powerful that it has become audible, exposing his secret.

TOP TIP!

Onomatopoeia is SUCH a tricky word to spell! You are not alone. I remember how to spell it by singing the letters to the tune of 'Old MacDonald had a farm… ee i ee i o'.

Rhetorical question

Definition: A question that doesn't require an answer.

Example: In *Romeo and Juliet*, the Friar asks Romeo, *'Art thou a man?'* Actually, there's repetition of rhetorical questions in his speech because he goes on to say, *'Hast thou slain Tybalt? Wilt thou slay thyself?'*, as he attempts to make Romeo reflect on the consequences of his impulsive behaviour.

In *Macbeth*, Lady Macbeth does the same thing – she challenges her husband's masculinity to try to convince him to kill the king by repeatedly asking him questions like, *'Was the hope drunk/ Wherein you dressed yourself?'*.

Okay. So that's our more basic devices done.

Learn them. Memorise them. Be them.

Let's move on to some higher-level stuff…

Oxymoron

Definition: When you have two words with opposite meanings next to each other or very close to each other, like 'bitter sweet', 'deafening silence', 'happily married' – joking!

Example: In *Romeo and Juliet*, when Romeo says, *'O brawling love, loving hate… cold fire, sick health…'*, the oxymorons show he is struggling to deal with his infatuation and inner conflict.

And in *Macbeth*, the witches chant *'Fair is foul, and foul is fair'*, which conveys their distorted morality. They cannot tell the difference between good and bad, and this links to the theme of appearance and reality.

Juxtaposition

Definition: When two things contrast with each other. In my head, it's a bit like an oxymoron… except an oxymoron is two opposite WORDS, whereas juxtaposition can be two characters that oppose each other, two settings that are different to each other, two paragraphs that have really different tones…

Example: In *Macbeth*, Shakespeare uses juxtaposition between Macbeth's treachery and Banquo's loyalty to show that it was possible to continue obeying the Divine Right despite the witches' prophecies; Macbeth's betrayal, therefore, was an act of free will, and not a result of fate or the supernatural.

Semantic field

Definition: A group of words that all link to the same topic or theme.

Example: In the poem 'Tissue', Dharker uses a semantic field of journeys, with words like *'maps'*, *'rivers'* and *'roads'*, cementing the idea that the poem is actually a metaphor for the man-made distance between people.

Colour imagery

Definition: When a writer mentions a colour to represent a deeper meaning.

Example: When Macbeth explains why he doesn't want to kill Duncan, he says, *'He hath honoured me of late, and I have bought/ Golden opinions from all sorts of people'*. Gold has connotations of something that's precious and pure. Macbeth is referring to all the praise he has received, and the colour imagery reflects how valued he feels.

If you spot a colour, for goodness' sake, please talk about it. Colour is one of the easiest things to analyse. People always say English teachers are extra and they analyse why the curtain was blue, when maybe the curtain was just blue. But that's NOT TRUE! Imagine if Voldemort came through the darkness to kill Harry… and he was wearing a YELLOW cape. It just wouldn't work, would it? It wouldn't match the tone. So, if you spot a colour, definitely talk about the colour imagery, explain what the connotations of that colour are and then link it to the question. It's easy marks.

Animal imagery

Definition: When something is compared to, or described as being like, an animal.

Example: In the poem 'The Charge of the Light Brigade', Tennyson says, *'Into the jaws of Death,/ Into the mouth of Hell'*. This makes the war seem wild and ferocious.

Religious imagery

Definition: When you use any word linking to religion. It doesn't have to be an OBVIOUSLY religious word like JESUS or GOD – religious imagery can be more symbolic like FIRE, because it has connotations of hell and punishment. Any words that remind you of religion can be called religious imagery.

Example: In *An Inspector Calls*, the Inspector says, *'if men will not learn that lesson, then they will be taught it in fire and blood and anguish.'* Perhaps Priestley is implying that capitalism is amoral and a sin, and that the Birling family will be punished if they do not change their ways.

Now, these last few devices are the most advanced. Are you ready?

Polysyndeton

Definition: The repetition of conjunctions – when the words 'and', 'so', 'or', 'but' are repeated.

Example: Did you notice how Priestley doesn't say they will be taught the lesson in *'fire, blood and anguish'*? He says… *'fire **AND** blood **AND** anguish'*. That repetition of the word 'and' is what we call POLYSYNDETON.

So, when other students talk about what the repetition of 'and' shows, YOU'RE going to say, *'the use of polysyndeton shows that the Inspector is warning the Birling family that if they do not change their selfish behaviour, the consequences will be long lasting and very severe.'*

Zoomorphism

Definition: When a human is given animal characteristics.

Example: In *The Strange Case of Dr Jekyll and Mr Hyde*, Hyde is presented as savage and uncivilised through the writer's use of zoomorphism in the quotation *'ape-like fury'*.

In *The Sign of Four*, Holmes is compared to birds and hounds when the writer says, *'… with his long thin nose only a few inches from the planks, and his beady eyes gleaming and deep-set like those of a bird'*, emphasising his instinctive nature.

Anthropomorphism

Definition: When an animal is given human characteristics (basically the opposite of zoomorphism).

Example: In *Macbeth*, Lady Macbeth uses anthropomorphism when she says, *'The raven himself is hoarse/ That croaks the fatal entrance of Duncan/ Under my battlements.'* Here, she's conveying the raven's excitement, as his voice has become *'hoarse'* by excitedly announcing Duncan's arrival. In this way, the bird, which typically forebodes death, mirrors Lady Macbeth's own anticipation.

Microcosm

Definition: When a character or object symbolises something bigger.

Example: In *An Inspector Calls*, Sheila symbolises something much bigger than just a young girl. She is a microcosm for the Suffrage movement. Priestley uses the way Sheila's character gains a voice and power as the play progresses to convey the message to the audience that they too can make a change and fix the mistakes that were made in the past.

Chremamorphism

Definition: When a human is given object qualities.

Example: In *A Christmas Carol*, Scrooge is described as *'hard and sharp as flint'*. Scrooge is a human... he is being compared to *'flint'* which is a rock, therefore that is not only a simile, but also chremamorphism. This makes it seem as though Scrooge lacks human empathy and emotions.

Right... that's enough for now. Remember, it's not just about spotting these devices and saying THIS IS ZOOMORPHISM. You need to be able to EXPLAIN what these devices show, what effect they create, and how they link to the text and the question.

And I'm going to teach you how to do all of that in this guide.

Let's get into it.

LANGUAGE PAPER 1 – OVERVIEW

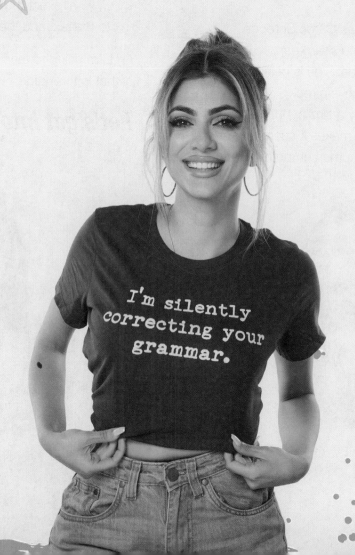

You have two English Language exams: Paper 1 and Paper 2. The English Language exams are different to your Literature exams because they aren't about a book or a poem that you have already studied in class. Instead, you have to answer questions on extracts that you've never seen before – and then you need to complete a writing task.

We're going to start by looking at Paper 1...

There are a few key things you need to know before we start looking at how to answer each individual question:

- The paper is 1 hour 45 minutes long.
- The paper is worth 80 marks in total.
- Paper ONE has ONE fiction extract you have to read.
- There are two sections: Section A is Reading; Section B is Writing.
- There are **four** questions in **Section A** (40 marks). These questions are about the extract.
- You answer **one** question from **Section B** (40 marks). You will have a CHOICE of two questions. This is where you write your own description or story.
- Generally, you spend **10–15 minutes** reading the extract. After that, the rule is 'a minute per mark'. (So, that means if Question 1 is worth 4 marks, you spend 4–5 minutes on it. Question 2 is 8 marks... you spend 8–10 minutes on it. And so on.)
- TIMINGS ARE SO IMPORTANT IN THIS EXAM. Most students run out of time in the Language exam. You MUST STICK TO TIMINGS RELIGIOUSLY. Even if you haven't finished the answer, move on. Otherwise, you end up wasting too much time on little 4 markers and 8 markers and run out of time for the BIG Questions 4 and 5, **which are worth more than half the marks of the whole paper**.
- You MUST practise doing a paper with timings before the real thing.

ACTIVE READING

When it comes to the Language paper, a lot of people panic because they're worried they won't understand the extract. That is fine and that is normal. Even I worry I won't understand the extract.

But you must remember my wise words:

- No one is expecting you to understand every single line.
- You don't *need* to understand every single line.
- As long as you can summarise what happens in every paragraph, and understand the main gist of what's going on, you'll be fine.

You have a solid 10–15 minutes to read the extract. Do NOT rush your reading time. Some students love to read as quickly as possible and get straight onto questions because they're scared of running out of time, but this is a mistake. You'll just end up missing important information or misunderstanding the extract, and then you won't answer the questions as well as you could have.

My most helpful tip is that you should read the extract TWICE… that's what I like to do. The first time, the words might not go in properly and you'll still be quite nervous. And then, the second time, you can actually start to absorb and understand what you are reading – and maybe even start labelling any language devices you find and anything else that stands out to you, like a really long or short paragraph or a section of dialogue.

A really good habit is to scribble down a couple of words on the side of each paragraph whilst you're reading, just summarising what's happening. This will only take about one extra minute in total, but it means you will process the extract better and not panic over a word or a sentence you don't fully understand. This is called ACTIVE READING.

But, if you do come across a word you don't understand, what can you do?

Here are a few things you can try:

1. Check if the word looks similar to another word that you know – they might come from the same root word and therefore have similar meanings. For example, if you don't understand the word 'audible', you might notice it is similar to the word 'audio'… and this might help you to figure out the definition.
2. Read the sentence before the one with the word in, read the sentence after, and then see if that helps you make more sense of it.
3. Try to read the sentence again, but just skip over the word you don't understand and then see if you can fill in the gap.

Here's the extract we're going to be working from…

If you want, you can practise my ACTIVE READING techniques before moving onto Question 1.

I've started you off and summarised what the first paragraph is about.

In this extract from a novel, Venus, a famous singer from the 1960s, is unable to accept how much she has aged. She remembers a time when she was young and beautiful.

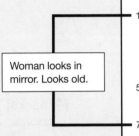

Woman looks in mirror. Looks old.

1 'I'm not old,' she whispered under her breath.

With one frail finger, the woman traced the outline of her reflection. There were deep, dark, dreadful lines engraved into her skin. Her nails were cracked, half bitten, half marked by the burden of age.

5 With slight trepidation, she lifted her heavy eyelids to look further up her arm. Her brownish skin seemed paler than usual; green veins

7 protruded like caterpillars crawling under her skin.

Conscious of her trembling hands, the old woman reached towards the glass trophy that sat balanced on her mantelpiece. The coldness

10 of its exterior startled her. She clenched onto it tightly, unable to bear the thought of it slipping from her sweaty palms. Unable to let the past go.

Beneath a layer of grey dust, the old woman could see her face trapped… imprisoned within the shiny surface. The wrinkles around

15 her eyes distorted their original beauty and form. Her lips were chapped, pursed, and her cheeks sunken in. Her flat, greasy hair hung like colourless strings. She drew in her breath sharply, asking the mirror silent questions.

19 Looking at her current state, it was almost impossible to imagine the
20 beauty she once possessed.

21 Once, she was Venus. Draped in a dress that was a deep azure in colour, it was as though midnight itself had swept around her. Twinkling stars shone out of the swathes of material, and the glitter cascaded behind her as she glided across the stage, like a

25 divine light. Her feet were blessed with clementine shoes and her body adorned with enchanting jewels. Falling in waves down her slender back, her long, blonde hair undulated to the rhythm of her movement; loose strands protected her porcelain face, guarding its perfection with fierce peacock pride. Her eyes sparkled like

30 diamonds, and were so blue that even poetry would have failed to capture their essence and depth; her eyes told a story and spoke to millions without uttering a single syllable. She smiled radiantly at her admirers. Her eyes opened wide as she reached the centre of the

34 stage, and she swung her hair back to get a full view of her award.

35 The glass trophy.

With a steady hand and stable fingers, she reached towards the prized possession. She displayed it with confidence and a natural ease. Cameras flashed incessantly, blinding her.

'I'm not old!' the old woman shrieked aloud. The noise shook

40 her frail fingers and the trophy slipped from her weak grip. As it hovered between the air and the ground, she closed her eyes and waited to hear the traumatising sound of smashing glass.

'I'm not old.'

Section A – QUESTION 1
4 marks, 5 minutes

The beauty of the Language paper is you always know what questions are going to come up – the questions never change. It's just the extract that changes. So, Question 1 will always be… LIST FOUR THINGS YOU LEARN ABOUT _____.

In our example paper, it's:

0	1	Read again the first part of the source, from **lines 1 to 7**.

List **four** things you learn about the woman in this part of the source. **[4 marks]**

This question really is as simple as it seems. They're not trying to trick you and they're not looking for deep answers. This question is just warming you up, checking if you understand English, testing whether you can read, if you understood the extract, and if you can select relevant quotations.

Now, I've taught this paper for a long, long time and there are a few things I see go wrong every year.

So, the things to keep in mind are:

- BE CAREFUL OF LINE NUMBERS. I know it sounds obvious, and I know you think it won't be you… but every single year someone leaves that exam hall and realises that they've selected information from the wrong lines. Don't let that be you.

- You've been asked to identify FOUR answers from the extract, so make sure you do four. Don't do five because you couldn't decide. Don't do three because you couldn't think of a fourth. Do FOUR.

- You are allowed to paraphrase (that means put quotations into your own words) or you can just select four quotations and copy them exactly how they are in the extract. Personally, I think selecting quotations is less risky so that's what I would suggest.

- Relevant quotations should be SELECTED – that means you can't just copy the whole of lines 1 to 7 and hope the answer is in there somewhere. And you can't make them too short either.

- Now here's the most important one. Do not use inference. There is no reading between the lines required for this question. If you try to be too clever and deep, you'll lose marks. Stick to the OBVIOUS facts.

- Make sure your answer is RELEVANT to the question.

> *Do not use inference. There is no reading between the lines required for this question.*

Now, because we are kings and queens...

We have to make sure we don't fall into any of these traps. So, the first thing we're going to do is, we will take a different coloured pen and draw a box around the lines given in the question (1–7):

> In this extract from a novel, Venus, a famous singer from the 1960s, is unable to accept how much she has aged. She remembers a time when she was young and beautiful.

1 'I'm not old,' she whispered under her breath.

With one frail finger, the woman traced the outline of her reflection. There were deep, dark, dreadful lines engraved into her skin. Her nails were cracked, half bitten, half marked by the burden of age.
5 With slight trepidation, she lifted her heavy eyelids to look further up her arm. Her brownish skin seemed paler than usual; green veins
7 protruded like caterpillars crawling under her skin.

Conscious of her trembling hands, the old woman reached towards the glass trophy that sat balanced on her mantelpiece. The coldness
10 of its exterior startled her. She clenched onto it tightly, unable to bear the thought of it slipping from her sweaty palms. Unable to let the past go.

Beneath a layer of grey dust, the old woman could see her face trapped… imprisoned within the shiny surface. The wrinkles around
15 her eyes distorted their original beauty and form. Her lips were chapped, pursed, and her cheeks sunken in. Her flat, greasy hair hung like colourless strings. She drew in her breath sharply, asking the mirror silent questions.

19 Looking at her current state, it was almost impossible to imagine the
20 beauty she once possessed.

21 Once, she was Venus. Draped in a dress that was a deep azure in colour, it was as though midnight itself had swept around her. Twinkling stars shone out of the swathes of material, and the glitter cascaded behind her as she glided across the stage, like a
25 divine light. Her feet were blessed with clementine shoes and her body adorned with enchanting jewels. Falling in waves down her slender back, her long, blonde hair undulated to the rhythm of her movement; loose strands protected her porcelain face, guarding its perfection with fierce peacock pride. Her eyes sparkled like
30 diamonds, and were so blue that even poetry would have failed to capture their essence and depth; her eyes told a story and spoke to millions without uttering a single syllable. She smiled radiantly at her admirers. Her eyes opened wide as she reached the centre of the
34 stage, and she swung her hair back to get a full view of her award.

35 The glass trophy.

With a steady hand and stable fingers, she reached towards the prized possession. She displayed it with confidence and a natural ease. Cameras flashed incessantly, blinding her.

'I'm not old!' the old woman shrieked aloud. The noise shook
40 her frail fingers and the trophy slipped from her weak grip. As it hovered between the air and the ground, she closed her eyes and waited to hear the traumatising sound of smashing glass.

'I'm not old.'

Done. ✓

Now, let's highlight what we are looking for in the question:

> **0 1** Read again the first part of the source, from **lines 1 to 7**.
>
> List **four** things you learn about the woman in this part of the source. **[4 marks]**

Next, let's write down *'The woman'* on the side of each answer line to make sure our answer stays relevant:

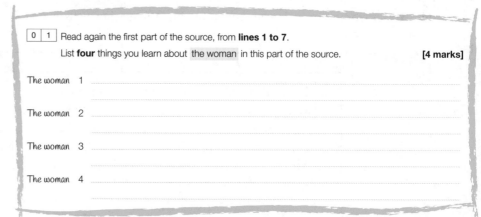

> **0 1** Read again the first part of the source, from **lines 1 to 7**.
>
> List **four** things you learn about the woman in this part of the source. **[4 marks]**
>
> The woman 1 ....
>
> The woman 2 ....
>
> The woman 3 ....
>
> The woman 4 ....

Then, we will re-read the given lines, stop after every sentence and see if there's anything relevant about the woman. If there is, highlight it.

> 1 'I'm not old,' she whispered under her breath.
> With one frail finger, the woman traced the outline of her reflection. There were deep, dark, dreadful lines engraved into her skin. Her nails were cracked, half bitten, half marked by the burden of age.
> 5 With slight trepidation, she lifted her heavy eyelids to look further up her arm. Her brownish skin seemed paler than usual; green veins
> 7 protruded like caterpillars crawling under her skin.

Finally, we need to pick our favourite FOUR quotations that are DEFINITELY ANSWERING THE QUESTION and ARE QUITE DIFFERENT TO EACH OTHER so we aren't repeating ourselves.

How do we do that?

Well, what about this one? The woman was sad.
Will that get a mark?
NO. Because I am trying to use inference and am reading between the lines! The woman might like being old. We don't know. We can't assume.

So, let's try again. The woman had trembling hands.
Are we happy with that answer?
NO. Because it's not from lines 1 to 7!

So, let's try one last time...

My final four answers are:

1 The woman 'traced the outline of her reflection'.
2 The woman's nails were 'cracked'.
3 The woman had 'brownish skin' which 'seemed paler than usual'.
4 The woman had 'green veins' protruding from under her skin.

4/4! Finally. But any four of the highlighted answers would have got us the mark.

RIGHT. We've secured our first 4 marks...

So, let's move on to Question 2.

TOP TIP!

Students often ask what happens if someone puts two correct answers from the same line of the extract together as one answer — like 'the woman's nails were cracked and half bitten.' A nice examiner would probably give you two marks... but try to separate your correct answers into four clear ideas.

Section A – QUESTION 2
8 marks, 10 minutes, 2 paragraphs

Remember I told you you'd need to know your language devices? Now is the time to start using them. Welcome to Question 2 – the language analysis question.

Question 2 will always begin with something like, HOW DOES THE WRITER USE LANGUAGE TO DESCRIBE... So, this is where you show off that you can identify a language device – like spot a simile – and then analyse its effect.

You already know what language devices are, but to do this question really well, you need to identify the most common word types too. Instead of saying, 'the WORD shows', it's better if you can identify the TYPE of word.

Some word types you should know are:

- **Noun:** a person, place or thing. Most of the time, you can ask yourself, 'Can I touch it?' If you can, it's a noun, e.g. *table.*
- **Proper noun:** the name of a person or a place; starts with a capital letter.
- **Abstract noun:** a feeling or emotion, a noun that you can't touch, e.g. *peace*
- **Adjective:** describes the noun, e.g. *hard table*
- **Verb:** doing word. Is it something you can do? If yes, it's a verb, e.g. *The hard table rested*
- **Adverb:** describes the verb. Usually ends in LY (but not always), e.g. *The hard table rested peacefully*
- **Personal pronoun**, e.g. *me, I*
- **Possessive pronoun**, e.g. *my, mine*
- **Inclusive pronoun**, e.g. *our, us, we*
- **Direct address**, e.g. *you, your*
- **Preposition:** a word that explains where something is, e.g. *under, over, behind, above, below*, etc.
- **Imperative:** commanding word

Here's the question we will be practising:

| 0 | 2 | Look in detail at this extract, from lines **21 to 34** of the source. |

How does the writer use language here to describe the young Venus?

You could include the writer's choice of:
- words and phrases
- language features and techniques
- sentence forms.

[8 marks]

For this question, they'll paste the bit they want you to look at, so you don't have to worry about line numbers. Let's highlight what we're looking for in the question:

| 0 | 2 | Look in detail at this extract, from lines **21 to 34** of the source.

How does the writer use language here to describe the young Venus ?

You could include the writer's choice of:
- words and phrases
- language features and techniques
- sentence forms.

[8 marks]

And now we need to re-read the extract and highlight any quotation which describes what young Venus was like. We have to make sure the quotations we select are JUICY and have an interesting language device that we can analyse, because that's the whole point of the question. I've highlighted and annotated the extract with some things that I found – there's loads in there.

dental plosive alliteration/colour imagery

simile

guttural alliteration/ simile/religious imagery

metaphor

personification

religious imagery

bilabial plosive alliteration/ personification

metaphor

personification

simile

colour imagery

Once, she was Venus. Draped in a dress that was a deep azure in colour, it was as though midnight itself had swept around her. Twinkling stars shone out of the swathes of material and the glitter cascaded behind her as she glided across the stage, like a divine light. Her feet were blessed with clementine shoes and her body adorned with enchanting jewels. Falling in waves down her slender back, her long, blonde hair undulated to the rhythm of her movement; loose strands protected her porcelain face, guarding its perfection with fierce peacock pride. Her eyes sparkled like diamonds, and were so blue that even poetry would have failed to capture their essence and depth; her eyes told a story and spoke to millions without uttering a single syllable. She smiled radiantly at her admirers. Her eyes opened wide as she reached the centre of the stage, and she swung her hair back to get a full view of her award.

Now remember, this is only an 8 marker...

So, you are not going to manage to write about ALL of these quotations in 8–10 minutes. We're only going to write TWO PARAGRAPHS and analyse TWO JUICY QUOTATIONS. To get full marks, we should try to analyse the effect of all three of the bullet points stated in the question: interesting words, language devices and sentence forms.

I could use, *'She smiled radiantly at her admirers'*... but then what would my explanation be? This shows that young Venus was confident? There's not much juice in that. It's definitely not going to get a top grade because I can't get very deep with it.

I guess I could use the quotation, *'draped in a dress that was a deep azure'*, and that has some devices in it... but I'm not sure how I would link the harsh sound of the dental plosive alliteration to what young Venus was like.

So, after thinking about it for a bit...

... I have decided the quotations I'm going to use are:

> 'the glitter cascaded behind her as she glided across the stage, like a divine light.'

I like this because it has a religious simile of the 'divine light' that makes young Venus seem angelic. Then, to zoom into one word (because the bullet points said I had to analyse interesting words), I could either look at the verb 'glided' or zoom into the noun 'glitter'. If I want to go really deep, I can explain the effect of the guttural alliteration, but I might not get time to do that in 8 minutes, which is okay.

> 'protected her porcelain face...'

In this quotation, the first and most important thing that stands out to me is the metaphor of her face being 'porcelain', and now that I think about it, I don't need to talk about the guttural alliteration in quotation 1 because instead, I could analyse the bilabial plosive alliteration in this quotation. There's no point talking about alliteration twice when I only have two paragraphs to show off to the examiner.

Now, we mustn't forget that we also need to talk about sentence structure, so I need to mention that most of the sentences in this extract are long and complex, and then link that to what young Venus was like.

So, what's next?

I'm going to give you a template that you can copy down, which will give you the sentence starters that you can then use to write your own two paragraphs in your exam. If you follow this structure, it will ensure you are hitting all three bullet points in the question:

Firstly, the writer uses language to present the young Venus as captivating: '... she glided across the stage, like a divine light.' Here, the use of the religious simile in 'divine light' gives the young Venus an elevated status beyond regular humans, and creates the impression that the young Venus' beauty was so powerful that she almost seemed angelic. Also, the use of the verb 'glided' emphasises her graceful movement, reinforcing her ethereal appearance.

Moreover, the writer uses language to present the young Venus as flawless: 'protected her porcelain face...'. Here, the metaphor of her 'porcelain face' suggests that her complexion is smooth and almost perfect — however, the writer could also subtly be hinting at the young Venus' fragility. The juxtaposition between the harsh sound created through the bilabial plosive alliteration and the weakness of 'porcelain' could perhaps imply that the young Venus had the appearance of confidence, but was in fact vulnerable. This idea of the young Venus being a complex character is reinforced by the fact that most of the sentences in this extract are long, which could symbolise the depth and layers to her personality.

So, if we break that down, I have:

1 Written two points that answer the question, using words from the question.
2 Selected two juicy quotations – not too long, not too short.
3 Identified some language devices and analysed their effects, linking back to the question (try not to repeat the same device in both paragraphs).
4 Zoomed in to an interesting word.
5 Analysed the sentence structure.

And, there you have it… Language Paper 1, Question 2, in the bag.

Section A – QUESTION 3
8 MARKS, 10 MINUTES, 3 PARAGRAPHS

Now, as we know, the Language paper is quite amazing because we already know what questions are going to come up. It's only the extract that changes. So, Question 3 will always be:

| 0 | 3 | You now need to think about the **whole** of the source. |

This text is taken from the beginning of a novel.

How has the writer structured the text to interest you as a reader?

You could write about:
- what the writer focuses your attention on at the beginning of the source
- how and why the writer changes this focus as the source develops
- any other structural features that interest you.

[8 marks]

It's the structure question! So, in the same way that you had to prove that you can identify a language device – like a simile or a metaphor – and analyse the effect in Question 2, you have to prove that you can identify STRUCTURAL techniques and analyse their effect for Question 3.

But what does that even mean?

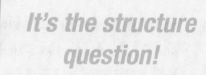

It's the structure question!

Everyone always hates Question 3 because they don't know what structural techniques they should be looking for. So let me tell you.

Some things you can look for are:
- **Foreshadowing** (when there is a hint that something will happen later in the extract)
- Long or short **paragraphs**
- A section of **dialogue** (speech)
- A **change in setting** (for example, if the beginning of the extract describes INSIDE a building and then in the middle it describes OUTSIDE the building)
- A **shift in tone** (like if the beginning of the extract is happy and then it becomes sad)
- An **introduction** to a main/new character
- A **flashback**
- A **cliffhanger**
- A **cyclical structure** (when the beginning of the extract is similar to the end of the extract)

I mean, technically, I don't even need to read the extract to attempt this question. I can literally look at the extract and start getting ideas about what I'm going to talk about just from what it looks like on the page. I can see where there's an extra-long or extra-short paragraph, or where there's a section of dialogue. And then when I look deeper and start re-reading, I can find even more things from my structural devices list.

Let me show you what I mean:

Starts with dialogue

Introduces main character

1 'I'm not old,' she whispered under her breath.

With one frail finger, the woman traced the outline of her reflection. There were deep, dark, dreadful lines engraved into her skin. Her nails were cracked, half bitten, half marked by the burden of age.

5 With slight trepidation, she lifted her heavy eyelids to look further up her arm. Her brownish skin seemed paler than usual; green veins protruded like caterpillars crawling under her skin.

Conscious of her trembling hands, the old woman reached towards the glass trophy that sat balanced on her mantelpiece. The coldness of its exterior startled her. She clenched onto it tightly, unable to bear the thought of it slipping from her sweaty palms. Unable to let the past go.

Beneath a layer of grey dust, the old woman could see her face trapped… imprisoned within the shiny surface. The wrinkles around her eyes distorted their original beauty and form. Her lips were chapped, pursed, and her cheeks sunken in. Her flat, greasy hair hung like colourless strings. She drew in her breath sharply, asking the mirror silent questions.

Looking at her current state, it was almost impossible to imagine the beauty she once possessed.

Longest paragraph/ flashback

Once, she was Venus. Draped in a dress that was a deep azure in colour, it was as though midnight itself had swept around her. Twinkling stars shone out of the swathes of material, and the glitter cascaded behind her as she glided across the stage, like a divine light. Her feet were blessed with clementine shoes and her body adorned with enchanting jewels. Falling in waves down her slender back, her long, blonde hair undulated to the rhythm of her movement; loose strands protected her porcelain face, guarding its perfection with fierce peacock pride. Her eyes sparkled like diamonds, and were so blue that even poetry would have failed to capture their essence and depth; her eyes told a story and spoke to millions without uttering a single syllable. She smiled radiantly at her admirers. Her eyes opened wide as she reached the centre of the stage, and she swung her hair back to get a full view of her award.

Short, one - or two-line paragraphs

35 The glass trophy.

With a steady hand and stable fingers, she reached towards the prized possession. She displayed it with confidence and a natural ease. Cameras flashed incessantly, blinding her.

'I'm not old!' the old woman shrieked aloud. The noise shook her frail fingers and the trophy slipped from her weak grip. As it hovered between the air and the ground, she closed her eyes and waited to hear the traumatising sound of smashing glass.

Cyclical structure

'I'm not old.'

Okay, this question is 8 marks – so remember, according to our minute per mark rule, I only have around 10 minutes. And in those 10 minutes, I'm going to write THREE paragraphs. But don't worry – they're not going to be super long!

I need a paragraph about the BEGINNING of the extract, one about the MIDDLE and one about the END. I have already labelled some of my ideas so now I can start writing…

Let's give it a go...

At the beginning of the extract, the writer focuses the reader's attention on the old woman and introduces her as the main character: '"I'm not old," she whispered under her breath.' Here, the writer uses dialogue right at the start to give readers an insight into the woman's fear of ageing even before they learn anything else about her. This is interesting for the reader because it makes them question who she is and how she ended up in this position.

In the middle of the extract, the writer shifts to a time when the old woman was younger: 'Once, she was Venus.' Here, the flashback reveals a contrasting image of a youthful and popular woman. This is interesting for the reader because they begin to understand what Venus' life was like before, helping them to appreciate why she is so unhappy now. The longest paragraph is used here, perhaps symbolising how Venus believed her youth and beauty would last forever, which the reader knows is not true.

Towards the end of the extract, the writer once again brings the reader's attention to how the old woman is struggling to cope with how different her life is now that she is older: '"I'm not old!" the old woman shrieked aloud.' Here, a cyclical structure is employed to perhaps symbolise how the old woman is trapped in her helplessness. This is interesting for the reader because it makes them feel empathetic towards the old woman, as she seems completely unable to accept the inevitability of ageing.

So, if we break that down, I have:

1. Written a point about the beginning, middle and end, explaining what's actually happening in those parts of the extract.

2. Selected a quotation that proves my point is true. It does NOT HAVE TO BE JUICY. Why? Because we aren't going to analyse the language in it. It's literally there to prove your point isn't a lie.

3. Identified a structural device in the same way I would spot a language device.

4. Explained the effect of that structural device.

5. Explained why that is interesting for the reader. What does it make them question or think or feel?

And there you have it…
Language Paper 1, Question 3.
Done and dusted.

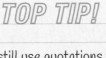

TOP TIP!

You must still use quotations to prove that your point is true – BUT DO NOT ANALYSE THE LANGUAGE DEVICES IN THEM. This isn't a language analysis question. It's about STRUCTURE. No one cares about similes or metaphors here.

TOP TIP!

You can use the wordings of Questions 1, 2 and 4 to help you start each paragraph of Question 3, as they tell you what each part of the extract is about. For example, Question 1 told me what the beginning of the extract was about, and that was basically a description of the old woman. So I said, 'At the beginning of the extract, the writer focuses the reader's attention on the old woman and introduces her as the main character.' Question 2 was about the young Venus, and that's what I wrote about in my middle paragraph. And (jumping forwards!), Question 4 is focused on the end of the extract, so I used it to help me write the point for my third paragraph in this question.

Section A – QUESTION 4
20 MARKS, 20 MINUTES, 3-4 PARAGRAPHS

Question 4 is a big one. It's a 20 marker (HALF OF THE WHOLE READING SECTION!) and it looks something like this:

---

0 4 Focus this part of your answer on the second half of the source, from **line 19 to the end**.

A student said, 'This part of the story shows the old woman is struggling to cope with how different her life is now that she is older and makes readers empathise with Venus.'

To what extent do you agree?

In your response, you could:

- consider your own impressions of Venus
- evaluate how the writer makes you empathise with her
- support your response with references to the text.

[20 marks]

So, the examiners basically give you a statement that they think is true, and they want you to write around THREE to FOUR paragraphs finding evidence that backs it up. If you want to, you could write two 'agree' paragraphs and one 'disagree'. But I would always make sure you are agreeing more than disagreeing.

It helps thinking about the Language paper as a whole – every question you've done so far has built up to this moment. In Question 1, they made you practise selecting quotations. In Question 2, they gave you a mini warm-up of looking for language devices and analysing them. Question 3 was about structure. And now, you're going to put it all together into one analytical essay.

Let's remind ourselves about the extract, line 19 to the end. As always, in the real exam, I would draw a box around those lines in a different coloured pen to make sure I don't accidentally write about the wrong lines.

---

19 Looking at her current state, it was almost impossible to imagine the
20 beauty she once possessed.

Once, she was Venus. Draped in a dress that was a deep azure in colour, it was as though midnight itself had swept around her. Twinkling stars shone out of the swathes of material, and the glitter cascaded behind her as she glided across the stage, like a
25 divine light. Her feet were blessed with clementine shoes and her body adorned with enchanting jewels. Falling in waves down her slender back, her long, blonde hair undulated to the rhythm of her movement; loose strands protected her porcelain face, guarding its perfection with fierce peacock pride. Her eyes sparkled like
30 diamonds, and were so blue that even poetry would have failed to capture their essence and depth; her eyes told a story and spoke to millions without uttering a single syllable. She smiled radiantly at her admirers. Her eyes opened wide as she reached the centre of the stage, and she swung her hair back to get a full view of her award.
35 The glass trophy.

With a steady hand and stable fingers, she reached towards the prized possession. She displayed it with confidence and a natural ease. Cameras flashed incessantly, blinding her.

'I'm not old!' the old woman shrieked aloud. The noise shook
40 her frail fingers and the trophy slipped from her weak grip. As it hovered between the air and the ground, she closed her eyes and waited to hear the traumatising sound of smashing glass.

'I'm not old.'

TOP TIP!

Because this question is worth SO many marks, these paragraphs are going to be WAY LONGER than any of the ones you wrote for Question 2 and Question 3.

Do you think Venus is struggling to cope? Do you feel sorry for her? Yes, I think so too. But how does the writer show this?

Let's pick our THREE JUICIEST quotations – that means quotations with interesting language or structural devices – to prove that she is struggling to cope and we empathise with her.

'The noise shook her frail fingers and the trophy slipped from her weak grip.'

I'm really excited to write about this one! I will analyse how the trophy is actually a microcosm of Venus's youth, and the fact that it's 'slipping' away from her shows how she is being forced to let go of her past self, even though she doesn't want to. I can mention the fricative alliteration too and link that to being a sad sound.

'"I'm not old!" the old woman shrieked aloud.'

I see an exclamation mark in her dialogue – so you know I'm going to talk about it. I can say that 'shrieked' is onomatopoeic. But also, it's ironic that she's screaming that she's '"not old!"', yet in the very same sentence, the narrative voice describes her as 'the old woman'.

'Her eyes sparkled like diamonds, and were so blue...'

Here, I'm going to talk about the simile of 'diamonds', and how valued she felt when she was younger. And then I can go in on the colour imagery of 'blue' (OBVS), exploring the connotations of the sky and sea. I'll link that to how Venus felt free when she was younger. I might bring in the fact that this is the longest paragraph too, so that I've analysed some structure.

Now that I've got my plan, I can start writing my paragraphs out.

Have a look at my model answer – you can use this as a template when you're writing your own paragraphs:

Firstly, I strongly agree that Venus is struggling to cope with how different her life is now and this is conveyed through the writer's use of contrast: 'Her eyes sparkled like diamonds, and were so blue ...'. Here, the simile comparing young Venus' eyes to 'diamonds' not only emphasises their beauty and radiance but also reflects how valued she felt when she was younger – as if her life had precious meaning. The colour imagery of 'blue' connotes the vastness of the sky and sea, which may be symbolic of how free Venus felt when she was younger, and the potential she felt she had. However, the comma in the middle of the sentence creates a pause, perhaps subtly implying that this beauty will not last forever. Structurally, her inability to accept her old age is reinforced through the fact that this description of her younger self is the longest paragraph; evidently, Venus is incapable of living in the present and escapes by remembering the past, proving that she is struggling to accept that she is no longer that glamorous woman she once was.

Furthermore, it can also be argued that the writer effectively emphasises Venus' struggle through the symbol of the glass trophy. The writer describes a powerful moment in which 'the noise shook her frail fingers and the trophy slipped from her weak grip.' Here, the glass trophy seems to be an apt microcosm of Venus' youth, and the fact that it's 'slipping' away from her shows how she is being forced to let go of her past self, even though she doesn't want to. The fricative alliteration in 'frail fingers' also creates a mournful tone – as if mirroring Venus' loss of energy and strength, emphasising her helplessness. Readers are forced to empathise with this character who is gripping onto an object she won in the prime of her youth, but the fact that it is made out of 'glass' is a brutal reminder of its temporary and fragile nature – showing how she is holding onto a vision of herself that cannot exist for long.

Moreover, I certainly agree that readers feel empathy for young Venus through the writer's use of dialogue: '"I'm not old!" the old woman shrieked aloud.' The writer uses an exclamation mark here to convey the pain and anguish in Venus' voice – and to portray her loss of control over her emotions. The verb 'shrieked' is onomatopoeic, which awakens the reader's senses and its harshness takes away from the confidence of her words – as if, subconsciously, she knows she is lying to herself too. It is also ironic that Venus is declaring that she's '"not old"', yet in the very same sentence, the narrative voice describes her as 'the old woman'. This epithet is a reminder that her age has become an engrained part of her identity and how the world sees her – and her denial of it reduces her to a figure of tragedy and pity. Clearly, the writer wants readers to empathise with Venus as her glamorous past only serves to reinforce why she is unable to accept the inevitability of time in her present state.

So, what I've done here for each paragraph is:

1. Written a point that answers the question, using words from the statement. Notice, I've mentioned a generic method in the point too – like 'through contrast', 'symbol', 'dialogue'. To get the highest marks, you should do this.

2. Selected a juicy quotation – not too long, not too short. Just enough to get some good juice from it.

3. Identified a language device or an interesting word choice and analysed the effect, linking back to the question. The explanation here is much LONGER than for previous questions because this question is worth MORE MARKS.

4. Given myself some extra marks by analysing a punctuation mark, where appropriate.

5. Reinforced my point by talking about structure.

6. Referred back to the statement.

It might seem like a lot, but if you use the same sentence starters as I have and practise with another extract, you'll feel a lot better about doing this yourself.

You've got this, I promise.

And that's the reading section done.
Well done, gang!
Let's get on to creative writing.

Section B – QUESTION 5 (The WRITING Section)

40 marks, 45 minutes, 1.5–2 pages

For more on this, see my video:

Right, it's time to move on to the creative writing section. This is where you will be asked to write a DESCRIPTION or a STORY.

I often suggest that students do this question first in the exam, before they attempt Questions 1, 2, 3 and 4. This is because this question alone is worth HALF THE MARKS of the whole Language paper, so we want to make sure you don't run out of time and end up rushing it. I would definitely suggest that you try to do a full paper in timed conditions before the real exam.

Use this method and see if it works for you:

- Read the extract to warm up your brain.
- Do Question 5 for 40–45 minutes.
- Read the extract again.
- THEN move onto the Reading section, Questions 1, 2, 3 and 4, IN THAT ORDER.

Question 5 will always look something like this:

| 0 | 5 | A magazine has asked for contributions for their creative writing page.

Either

Write a description of an isolated place as suggested by this picture:

or

Write a story with the title 'The Waiting Room'.

(24 marks for content and organisation
16 marks for technical accuracy)

[40 marks]

So, where do you start?

Remember, your examiner has HUNDREDS of scripts to mark. So, you want to make sure your writing STANDS OUT. Think outside the box – whose perspective are you going to write from? How can you make your writing different from everyone else's?

I once gave my students the above question (Write a story with the title 'The Waiting Room') and nearly all of them wrote about a hospital waiting room… which is fine… but after reading the thirtieth hospital description, it got quite boring. And then… one of my students wrote this:

Occasionally, I wonder what happens after death. Where do we go? Is it a Midas-kissed, utopian paradise where one resides, or a damp, dark, dungeon of doom… or neither? Regardless of where we end up in the afterlife – if it even exists – what confuses me is how, and where, our eternal destiny is decided. After some supernatural being weighs our soul for all its good and bad, where do we go to anxiously await the results?

The waiting room.

It is heaven and hell; light and dark; pain and ecstasy. It is purity and corruption; bliss and danger; joy and devastation. It is all of these things mashed together into one colossal purgatory.

Neatly dispersed across the space, sapphire chairs line the floor of the hall. They drip with luxury, yet they're sunken and deflated as if their egos have been hurt. Majestic chandeliers adorn the ceiling and ooze heavenly light, but some of the bulbs are flickering. Mighty stained-glass windows force a kaleidoscope of colours to cascade across the walls, but the cracks in the panes let the rain in; a puddle forms below, creating a pool of holy water for people to host any last-minute baptisms in, to optimise their chances of obtaining a place in heaven.

You would imagine that such a divine place would have the power to put people at peace – to shatter their sins with serenity – yet even the faintest wisp of wind from this room is enough to fill every pixel of every person's skin with fear.

And now I'm here.

As each of the chairs fill up one by one, my peripheral vision is filled with quivering legs and fidgeting fingers. Breaths speed up, as though everyone's lungs are desperately attempting to heave their transgressions out of their bodies. The stench of sweat is heavy in the air, suffocating the atmosphere with nerves and wrongdoings. My gaze shifts from one anxious visitor to another, as I juggle my judgements, calculating in which realm I perceive them to belong. Heaven, hell… or somewhere in between.

But then it hits me.

Where do I fit in? Yes, I have of course made mistakes, but have I made too many to be worthy of redemption? I am not evil, but am I good enough? What was my last good deed? When was my last crime? And even if I am guiltless, will He still declare me guilty?

Then I hear it. My name.

How brilliant is that?

The student took the task of the waiting room and described an imaginary place where people wait before God decides if they are going to heaven or hell.

Another standout piece I marked was about a family hiding in a house during a war, WAITING to see if they would survive. So again, it wasn't LITERALLY a waiting room. They did something a bit different.

Don't worry if this all seems scary...

If you can't think of a super original idea, you can always start by describing the **sky** and the **weather**. That's my trick. I nearly always start by describing the sky and weather (as long as it links to the question). What colour is the sky? Are there clouds? Is there a moon? Is it hiding behind the clouds? Is there a sun? A wild, howling wind? A gentle breeze? Fog? There is SO much to say – you can really show off your descriptive skills right from the beginning, and set the tone and the atmosphere of the piece.

If I were giving that first question a go, I would start with something like this:

> Write a description of an isolated place as suggested by this picture
>
> I was surrounded by beauty.
>
> Slowly, the fresh morning sun rose into the cloudless, azure sky; clumps of snowdrops gradually dissipated and the fresh, green finery of spring came to life. Ivory clouds undulated across the endless abyss, and a layer of scintillating fog separated the sky from the land. The starkness of winter had given way to spring as the last remnants of the cold melted away.
>
> Chaffinches and swans emerged from their hibernation to bask in the warm rays of the sun and, inspired by them, bees and butterflies flitted from flower to flower; they seemed to be gathering nourishment from the poppies, chrysanthemums and tulips that were unfurling their delicate petals.

After that, if you're stuck where to go next with your description, you can label the picture with all the other things you can see to help you.

TOP TIP!

NEVER, EVER END WITH 'It was all a dream'. We are not in primary school.

Here is a formula you can use for both stories and descriptions:

- Start with a one-line paragraph.
- Describe the sky and the weather in detail.
- Introduce a character. Describe where they are – what do the surroundings look like?
- If possible, think of a twist – something unexpected happens. KEEP IT SIMPLE… this isn't a Hollywood movie, so you don't need a massive storyline and loads of characters. There just needs to be a small change like a storm comes… or she sees a car in the distance… Leave it subtle and ambiguous.
- End with a one-line paragraph, similar to the opening line, so it's a cyclical structure!

If you are answering the first question, remember that the picture they give you is just a prompt, so you DON'T have to stick to ONLY WHAT YOU SEE IN THERE. Use your imagination and add your own details, using the picture as a starting point!

Let's get deeper into it…

Now, you can be Roald Dahl and write the best creative writing in the world, but there are certain things the examiner will be looking for in this question that you need to include in order to hit the mark scheme. We can break that mark scheme down into **eight simple bullet points**.

Use these points (given on the next page) like a checklist. Do not step out of your exam without making sure you have included all of these things in your writing.

Your creative writing is like a **cake**… and these are the ingredients you need to put into your cake to make it as yummy as possible!

Now, let's work through it...

Let's look at each of these skills one by one and make sure you know how to do them.

1. Sophisticated vocabulary

Because we aren't basic, we're not going to use boring, basic words. Here are some tricks you can use to make your vocabulary seem higher level:

- Use SOPHISTICATED COLOURS instead of basic colours. Rather than saying 'red', say 'crimson'. Instead of saying 'green', say 'emerald'. You'll notice in 'The Waiting Room', the student describes 'sapphire chairs' instead of saying 'blue'. In the 'isolated place' description, there is an 'azure sky' and 'ivory clouds'.

- It's a really good idea to mention a specific TYPE of bird instead of just saying 'birds', e.g. 'Chaffinches and swans emerged...'.

- In the same way, instead of just saying 'flowers', name the TYPE of flower, e.g. 'poppies, chrysanthemums and tulips'.

- If you can throw in the name of ONE character from Greek mythology, do it! You'll notice the phrase 'Midas-kissed' in 'The Waiting Room'. This is referring to King Midas – everything he touched turned to gold, so it basically means 'golden'.

> **TOP TIP!**
>
> As much as we love sophisticated vocabulary, we also don't want it to sound like you've swallowed a thesaurus and are vomiting it all over the page. Don't squash TOO many HUGE words all into one sentence, so that it loses all meaning and effect.

2. Language devices

I love language devices. When I'm writing, I stop before every sentence and think about whether I could turn it into a metaphor or a simile, etc. If you go back to the 'The Waiting Room' example and label every device you can find, you'll notice it's packed with devices EVERYWHERE.

So, in your exam...

I want you to make sure your writing includes:

- Personification
- Metaphor
- Simile
- Rhetorical question
- Onomatopoeia
- Alliteration/sibilance
- Rule of three
- Oxymoron
- Mythological/religious imagery
- Repetition

Let's continue the 'isolated place' description:

- **Personification:** Nature had awoken from its wintry slumber.
- **Metaphor:** I stood still, absorbing every pixel of the perfect painting. (See how I sneaked some alliteration in there too!)
- **Simile:** Gently, dewdrops floated in the cool air, before eventually decorating the ground like fragments of diamonds on the finest Indian silk.
- **Onomatopoeia:** Mixing with the melody of the gentle breeze, robins whistled and sang happy jingles, ready for the promise of a new season.
- **Religious imagery:** God was conducting the perfect orchestra.
- **Repetition:** It was beautiful – absolutely beautiful.
- **Oxymoron:** The silence was deafening.
- **Rule of three:** I sighed... I gasped... I screamed.
- **Rhetorical question:** How did I end up here?

3. One line of dialogue

In a description, it isn't necessary to include dialogue – but when you're writing a STORY, you should include someone speaking. You don't want to include LOADS of dialogue between characters. This is not a play. This is an exam and you want to get maximum marks by spending more time on your DESCRIPTIVE BITS. The maximum I will allow you is TWO LINES of dialogue if you absolutely HAVE to… but please don't get carried away.

I quite like to have a character talk to themselves. Like:

'This is incredible,' he whispered under his breath.

Now, what we don't want is for you to end up LOSING marks because you didn't punctuate your dialogue correctly.

So, the rules are:

- You need a capital letter to start the dialogue.
- The bit after the dialogue where you say 'he said' does NOT need a capital letter.
- All punctuation goes INSIDE the speech marks.
- When a new character speaks, it goes on a NEW LINE.

> **You don't want to include LOADS of dialogue between characters. This is not a play.**

4. & 5. Sentence structure

It would be really boring if every sentence you wrote started with THE THE THE THE. And it would also be really boring if all of your sentences were the same length. You need to include a mixture of long, descriptive sentences, and then mix that up with some short, dramatic sentences. You also need to make sure you are starting your sentences in different ways.

TOP TIP!

Try to include a one-word sentence in there somewhere.

Let's look at some different types of sentences:

A **simple sentence** is the same as a MAIN CLAUSE:

The stars were glistening.

Lovely. Simple. No comma. Makes sense by itself.

A **complex sentence** is made up of a main clause and a subordinate clause. A subordinate clause is a bit of extra information that doesn't make sense by itself. It needs a comma. Like this:

In the sky, the stars were glistening.

There are different types of subordinate clauses you can start your sentences with. Let me give you some options:

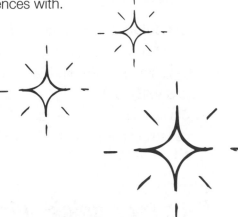

- Start with WHERE something is (a PREPOSITION):
  In the obsidian sky, the stars were glistening.
- Start with WHEN something happened:
  After the sun had set, the stars were glistening.
- Start with an ADVERB (-ly):
  Radiantly, the stars were glistening.
- Start with a VERB (-ing):
  Watching the world below, the stars were glistening.

Subordinate clauses don't just go at the start of your sentences, they can go at the end too:
The stars were glistening, watching the world below.

When you get good at this, subordinate clauses can split the main clause apart and go in the middle, with what I like to call a **comma sandwich**:
The stars, watching the world below, were glistening.

And when you become super clever, you can put the subordinate clause at the beginning AND the end of the sentence, to create extra-long sentences:
Radiantly, the stars were glistening, watching the world below.

Let's highlight the main and subordinate clauses in the section we just wrote, to make sure we have a mixture of both in different places:

Nature had awoken from its wintry slumber. I stood still, absorbing every pixel of the perfect painting. Gently, dewdrops floated in the cool air, before eventually decorating the ground like fragments of diamonds on the finest Indian silk. Under the melody of the gentle breeze, robins whistled and sang happy jingles, ready for the promise of a new season. God was conducting the perfect orchestra.

6. A range of sophisticated punctuation

There are two parts to this. Firstly, you need to make sure you are using a RANGE of punctuation in your writing – which means at least FIVE DIFFERENT TYPES of punctuation – and secondly, you need to make sure some of those are HIGHER-LEVEL PUNCTUATION MARKS.

So, what exactly does this mean?

Basically, you need to use:

1. • **Full stops** to mark the end of the sentence.

2. , **Commas** to show pauses (and to separate main and subordinate clauses).

3. ? A **question mark** when you write a rhetorical question.

4. " **Speech marks** in your one line of dialogue.

That's four… now let me tell you about the more sophisticated punctuation marks I would like you to use in an ideal world:

5. ; A **semicolon**. This bad boy MUST BE USED in your writing. There are two rules to using a semicolon correctly:
   - Both sentences on either side of the semicolon must be about the SAME TOPIC.
   - Both sentences on either side of the semicolon must be main sentences that MAKE SENSE ON THEIR OWN.

Let's try a quick quiz...

Correct or incorrect?

The rain was pouring; swimming is very fun.

INCORRECT – the sentences are not about the same topic

The rain was pouring; it was banging against my window.

CORRECT – the sentences are about the same topic AND make sense on their own

As I looked into the distance; I noticed the blurry outline of the dilapidated house.

INCORRECT – if you cover each side of the semicolon, they aren't both main sentences. Imagine if someone came up to you and said 'Hey… as I looked into the distance.' It wouldn't make sense, would it?

The ocean was stunning under the moonlight; moving, waving, crashing.

INCORRECT – 'moving, waving, crashing,' is not a main sentence!

I could turn this last one into the correct use of the semicolon by making a slight change: *The ocean was stunning under the moonlight; it was moving, waving and crashing.*

6 **– A dash.** A dash is a bit easier to use, because it doesn't have to have full sentences on each side. Let me give you some rules about using a dash:

- The EASIEST way to use a dash is with repetition at the end of a sentence. Like this:
  It was beautiful – absolutely beautiful.

- You can also use it before a conjunction (AND, BUT, OR, SO) – like an afterthought. Like this:
  I knew I shouldn't have followed him – but I couldn't help myself.

- If you're feeling really confident, you can replace commas or brackets and use two dashes for parenthesis – so adding extra information in the middle of a sentence. For example:
  I knew – or I hoped – that I would pass my exams.
  The boy – who seemed lost and frightened – cowered in the corner of the room.

> Don't worry if this last one confuses you – just use the dash in the first way and it gets the job done!

7 **...** I think an **ellipsis** is the easiest punctuation mark to use, because there aren't really any rules about how to use it. You just add it in wherever you want a dramatic pause... DUN DUN DUNNNN!

Have a think... where would you put the ellipsis in the following sentence?
I stepped forward and that's when I saw him.

Well, it could go here:
I stepped forward... and that's when I saw him.

That's quite a good, dramatic place for a pause, right? Or how about here:
I stepped forward and that's when... I saw him.

Yep. That works too. Let me give you another option:
I stepped forward and that's when I saw... Mehreen.

So, these are all the punctuation marks I want you to make sure you are using for this question.

You may have noticed I didn't include exclamation marks, brackets and colons. You can use them if you like... I just don't love them in descriptive writing. It's just a personal preference, but I'll leave that up to you.

7. Long and short paragraphs

You may already know that your writing needs to include paragraphs... The examiner wants to see that you can separate your ideas, and structure your work so it flows from paragraph to paragraph.

BUT I don't JUST want you to paragraph. I want you to use a mixture of long and short paragraphs to create specific effects.

Hear me out:

I once had a student who wrote a descriptive piece about an old man who was dying. At the beginning, when the man was healthy, the paragraph was the longest. And as the story went on and the man got weaker and sicker, the paragraphs got shorter. Until eventually, the piece ended on a one-line paragraph. Do you see why that's clever? The size of the paragraphs reflects what's happening in the story.

This might seem difficult to do in an exam when you're trying to think on the spot...

So, let me give you a trick:

The easiest way to show the examiner you know how to structure for effect is to use a CYCLICAL STRUCTURE in your creative writing. This means... match the OPENING of your description/story to the ENDING. Start and end with a similar line. Something like this:

Opening line: Lights filled the sky.

Ending line: Lights filled the sky — but the world remained dark.

Love that! A little oxymoron action for ya. Or, how about this one:

Opening line: I knew I would find her here.

Ending line: "I knew I would find you here."

We love the drama! This example ends on the one-line of dialogue which creates so much suspense.

Opening line: Silence. Serenity. Safety.

Ending line: The silence had been broken. The serenity had been shattered. And I knew... no one could save me now.

This is one of my favourite structures because it has a rule of three AND sibilance AND one-word sentences right at the beginning. So, the examiner will definitely be like... WOAH!

8. Technical accuracy

Obviously, you're not going to get a top grade if your writing has loads of spelling mistakes and the tenses are all over the place. 16 of your marks are based around your technical accuracy. That's a lot. So, you need to make sure you spend at least 5 minutes checking your work at the end.

Now if we put EVERYTHING I HAVE JUST TAUGHT YOU together, we end up with a piece of writing that looks something like this:

TOP TIP!

Stick to past tense. Students who try to write in present tense ('He is') always end up slipping into past ('He was')... so just stick to past.

I was surrounded by beauty.

Slowly, the fresh morning sun rose into the cloudless, azure sky; clumps of snowdrops gradually dissipated and the fresh, green finery of spring came to life. Ivory clouds undulated across the endless abyss, and a layer of scintillating fog separated the sky from the land. The starkness of winter had given way to spring as the last remnants of the cold melted away.

Chaffinches and swans emerged from their hibernation to bask in the warm rays of the Midas-kissed sun and, inspired by them, bees and butterflies flitted from flower to flower; they seemed to be gathering nourishment from poppies, chrysanthemums and tulips that were unfurling their delicate petals.

Nature had awoken from its wintry slumber. I stood still, absorbing every pixel of the perfect painting. Gently, dewdrops floated in the cool air, before eventually decorating the ground like fragments of diamonds on the finest Indian silk. Mixing with the melody of the gentle breeze, robins whistled and sang happy jingles, ready for the promise of a new season. God was conducting the perfect orchestra. It was beautiful – absolutely beautiful. The silence was deafening. I sighed... I gasped... I screamed.

How did I end up here?

My call for help pierced through the empty air and travelled far into the distance, finally reaching the rivulet that was undulating peacefully between the mossy rocks. I stumbled over to it, crushing the life that lay beneath my feet along the way. The water looked even clearer close up, the waves moving in harmony with the wind. I bent down to take a closer look, but what looked back at me was a monstrous sight.

Monstrous.

The girl looking back at me was someone I didn't even recognise. Her eyes were bloodshot red, and her porcelain skin stained with tears; deep scratches created a mosaic of pain and suffering along her tiny ankles, as evidence of the bristles and thorns she had passed through to get here. Her hair, pulled and beaten by the weather, now hung around her face, defeated. The sight of her bedraggled body created a stark contrast to the serene scenery that engulfed her.

She was surrounded by beauty – but she had never felt more alone.

Wow... stunning. I don't know about you, but reading a good piece of creative writing genuinely excites me. Why don't you find a picture and try to write your own piece using everything you have learnt?

And then... that's ONE. WHOLE. PAPER. DONE! ✓

LANGUAGE PAPER 2 – OVERVIEW

Remember, you have two English Language exams: Paper 1 and Paper 2. The English Language exams are different to your Literature exams because they aren't about a book or a poem that you have already studied in class. Instead, you have to answer questions on extracts that you've never seen before – and then you need to complete a writing task.

Welcome to Paper 2! Before we start looking at how to answer each question, there are a few things you need to know:

- The paper is 1 hour 45 minutes long.
- The paper is worth 80 marks in total.
- Paper 2 has TWO non-fiction extracts you have to read: **Source A** and **Source B**.
- One of the sources will be from the 19th century, and one will be modern.
- You answer all **four** questions from **Section A** (40 marks). These questions are about the **two extracts**.
- In **Section B** (the **writing** section) there is ONLY ONE QUESTION. YOU DO NOT GET A CHOICE.
- The timings rule is the same as Paper 1. You spend about **10–15 minutes** reading the extracts. After that, the rule is 'a minute per mark'.
- You MUST STICK TO TIMINGS RELIGIOUSLY. Even if you haven't finished the answer, move on. Just like Paper 1, **Question 4 and 5 are worth more than half the marks of the whole paper**, so you do NOT want to run out of time.
- You MUST practise doing a paper with timings before the real thing.

I'll say it again, a lot of people panic because they're worried they won't understand the extracts. That is fine and that is normal. Especially in Paper 2, where one of the extracts is from 'the olden days' and is obviously trickier to understand. But remember, no one is expecting you to understand every single line. You don't need to. As long as you can summarise what is happening in every paragraph… you're fine.

In the real exam, just like Paper 1, don't forget to do ACTIVE READING. Read the extracts TWICE and make notes to make sure you haven't missed any important information. (See page 16.)

> *No one is expecting you to understand every single line.*
>
> *As long as you can summarise what is happening in every paragraph… you're fine.*

Here are the two sources that we're going to be working from:

Source A

This extract is from a speech by teacher Mehreen Baig (me!), who describes the importance of women getting an education. It was delivered in 2017.

1 As I stand here before you today, some people will have assumptions of my ability – because I'm a woman. They will think that a man will be able to do a job better than me – simply because of my gender. They will even pay a man more than they pay me. In fact, the Office for National Statistics figures show that the gender pay gap for
5 workers in the UK currently stands at 18.1%. Hence the undeniable truth is that as women, we are immediately at a disadvantage. So how can we change this? How can we shatter these perceptions so that, one day, when we have daughters, they are truly given equal opportunities and are treated with the equal respect and dignity that they deserve?

10 I know there are many social and cultural expectations that discourage us from becoming too educated or too independent. In many households, we are brought up knowing that our ultimate goal in life is to get married. So many girls, despite being bright, talented and full of potential, grow up searching for a rich husband who can support and provide for them. But why don't we teach our girls how to look after
15 themselves?

I refuse to watch the young women I teach be reduced to their physical appearance or be treated as roti*-making machines. I want to teach my students how to challenge and defend themselves against the stereotypes and pitfalls that they will encounter on a daily basis. I want to give them the keys to open the doors of opportunity that
20 would otherwise remain locked or closed. I want to create such a solid foundation for them that no one can ever tell them they are reaching too high.

*a flat bread

Source B

The following article from *Punch*, titled 'The Best Sewing-Machine', is from 1859. The writer explains what qualities he admires in women.

1 The very best Sewing-Machine a man can have is a Wife. It is one that requires but a kind word to set it in motion, rarely gets out of repair, makes but little noise, is seldom the cause of dust, and, once in motion, will go on uninterruptedly for hours, without the slightest trimming, or the smallest personal supervision being necessary. It will

5 make shirts, darn stockings, sew on buttons, mark pocket handkerchiefs, cut out pinafores, and manufacture children's frocks out of any old thing you may give it; and this it will do behind your back just as well as before your face. In fact, you may leave the house for days, and it will go on working just the same. If it does get out of order a little, from being overworked, it mends itself by being left alone for a short time,

10 after which it returns to its sewing with greater vigour than ever. Of course, sewing machines vary a great deal. Some are much quicker than others. It depends in a vast measure upon the particular pattern you select. If you are fortunate in picking out the choicest pattern of a Wife—one, for instance, that sings whilst working, and seems to be never so happy as when the husband's linen is in hand—the Sewing-Machine

15 may be pronounced perfect of its kind; so much so, that there is no make-shift in the world that can possibly replace it, either for love or money. In short, no gentleman's establishment is complete without one of these Sewing-Machines in the house!

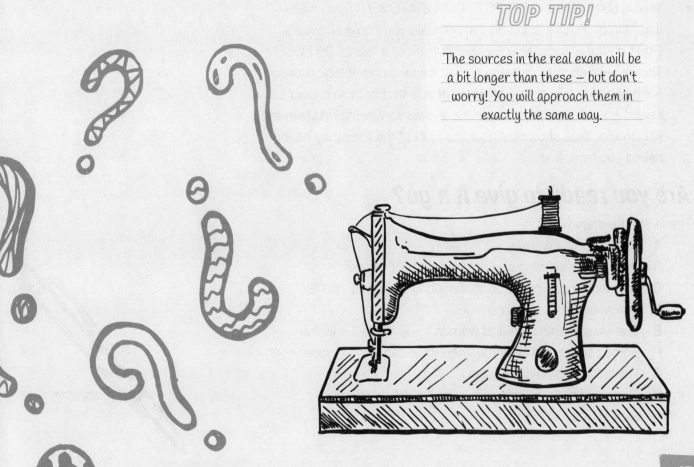

TOP TIP!

The sources in the real exam will be a bit longer than these — but don't worry! You will approach them in exactly the same way.

Section A – QUESTION 1
4 marks, 5 minutes

The beauty of the Language papers is that we always know what questions are going to come up. So, Question 1 for Paper 2 will always be…

CHOOSE FOUR STATEMENTS BELOW WHICH ARE TRUE.

It's a 4 marker, so we have a maximum of 5 minutes to answer.
For this example paper, the exact question is:

| 0 | 1 | Read again the first part of **Source A** from **lines 1 to 15**.

Choose **four** statements below which are **true**. **[4 marks]**

Now, this is slightly different from Paper 1 because you DON'T have to FIND AND SELECT QUOTATIONS – they actually give you the statements. This technically sounds easier… but I've taught this paper for many years and there are a few things I see go wrong all the time.

So, the things to keep in mind are:

- BE CAREFUL OF LINE NUMBERS. I know it sounds obvious, and I know you think it won't be you… but every single year someone selects an answer from the wrong line numbers. So, draw a box around the lines they have given you to avoid that from happening. Do that now please with Source A.

- You've been asked to SELECT FOUR STATEMENTS, so make sure you do FOUR. Don't do five because you couldn't decide. Don't do three because you couldn't think of a fourth. Do FOUR.

- The statements they give you should follow a chronological order, so the answer to whether **statement A** is true or false should be near the START of the extract. The answer to whether **statement H** is true or false should be near the END of the lines they have asked you to look at.

Are you ready to give it a go?

These are the statements:

- **A** The writer is a woman.
- **B** The writer feels men can do a job better than her.
- **C** The gender pay gap around the world stands at 18.1%.
- **D** The writer has a daughter.
- **E** The writer wants men and women to be treated equally.
- **F** Some people don't want women to become too independent.
- **G** The writer has a rich husband.
- **H** The writer believes girls should be taught to look after themselves.

A **The writer is a woman**. *'… because I'm a woman.'* ✓

B **The writer feels men can do a job better than her.** *'THEY will think that a man will be able to do a job better than me – simply because of my gender.'* ✗

Other people may think this – not the writer.

C **The gender pay gap around the world stands at 18.1%.** *'… the Office for National Statistics figures show that the gender pay gap for workers IN THE UK currently stands at 18.1%.'* ✗

It's in the UK – not the world!

D **The writer has a daughter.** *'How can we shatter these perceptions so that, ONE DAY, when we have daughters…'* ✗

This is not as obvious, but the fact that it says 'one day' IMPLIES that she does not have a daughter yet.

E **The writer wants men and women to be treated equally.** *'… they are truly given EQUAL opportunities and are treated with the EQUAL respect and dignity THAT THEY DESERVE?'* ✓

F **Some people don't want women to become too independent.** *'I know there are many social and cultural expectations that DISCOURAGE US FROM BECOMING too educated or TOO INDEPENDENT.'* ✓

G **The writer has a rich husband.** *'So many girls… grow up searching for a rich husband'* ✗

This is unfortunately false… but I am working on it!
The extract is talking in GENERAL about lots of girls growing up searching for a rich husband… but nowhere does it mention that the WRITER has a rich husband. We can't assume information that we don't have evidence for.

H **The writer believes girls should be taught to look after themselves.**
'… why don't we teach our girls how to look after themselves?' ✓

Easy peasy. First 4 marks secured.
Let's move on to Question 2.

Section A – QUESTION 2
8 marks, 10 minutes, 2 paragraphs

For Question 2, you need to look at BOTH extracts. The question will always be a SUMMARY OF DIFFERENCES or a SUMMARY OF SIMILARITIES.

In this example paper, the question is:

---

0 2   You need to refer to **Source A** and **Source B** for this question.

Both sources describe how women in society are treated.

Use details from **both** sources to write a summary of what you understand about the similar ways women are treated.

[8 marks]

It's an 8 marker, so we're spending a maximum of 10 minutes here. We're going to write TWO paragraphs – one about how women are treated in Source A, and one about how women are treated in Source B.

Look at the question carefully – it is asking you for a SUMMARY – so there is NO LANGUAGE ANALYSIS. We actually need to keep our explanations as SHORT AS POSSIBLE.

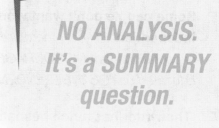

NO ANALYSIS.
It's a SUMMARY
question.

So, let's think…

In Source A, how are women treated? Are they treated in the same way as men? Are they always encouraged to get high flying jobs and be super independent? No.

Okay… so let's write our point:

In Source A, we learn that women are treated unequally compared to men:

Perfect.

Let's add a quotation to support this:

In Source A, we learn that women are treated unequally compared to men: '… the gender pay gap for workers in the UK currently stands at 18.1%.'

Time to add an explanation:

In Source A, we learn that women are treated unequally compared to men: '… the gender pay gap for workers in the UK currently stands at 18.1%.' Here, the use of the statistic shows…

Wait. No. NO ANALYSIS. It's a SUMMARY question.

Let's cross that out… and try again:

In Source A, we learn that women are treated unequally compared to men: '… the gender pay gap for workers in the UK currently stands at 18.1%.' This suggests that women are discriminated against in the workplace and are at a 'disadvantage' due to the misguided perception that men are 'able to do the job better' than women. Society and culture both undervalue women and treat men more favourably.

Do you see what I did in that explanation? I kept it short – only two sentences long – but in it, I embedded two other mini quotations.

Now, let's try all of that again with Source B:

Similarly, in Source B, we learn that women are undervalued and treated as inferior to men: 'The very best Sewing-Machine a man can have is a Wife.' This suggests that women are viewed as objects, particularly after they get married. They are only valued for their domestic work and ability to make as 'little noise' as possible so they don't disturb the important work of their 'husbands'. Therefore, although both texts recognise the 'vigour' and potential women have, they show that the women never get the opportunity to utilise it to its full potential.

Let's break down what I've done there:

1. I wrote a point that answers the question, using words from the question.

2. I selected a quotation (this did NOT HAVE TO BE JUICY because I wasn't going to analyse it).

3. I wrote a short explanation – one or two sentences long – but EMBEDDED two quotations in there.

4. I COMPARED the two sources. My second paragraph starts with a comparative word like SIMILARLY or IN CONTRAST, and at the end, I have a final evaluative sentence comparing both texts.

That wasn't too bad was it?
Let's move onto the bigger mark questions.

Section A – QUESTION 3
12 marks, 15 minutes, 3 paragraphs

For more on this, see my video:

Shall I tell you the best news ever? You have already learnt how to do this question. That's right – Language Paper 2, Question 3 is the SAME as Paper 1, Question 2!

It's HOW DOES THE WRITER USE LANGUAGE TO DESCRIBE…

The only difference is that in Paper 1, this question was only worth 8 marks, so we wrote two paragraphs… but here it's worth 12 marks, so we're going to spend a bit more time on it and write THREE paragraphs if possible.

Let's see if we can give that a go:

In this example question, we're looking at Source B. It's an 'olden days' text, so it's a bit more tricky to understand… but we only need to find THREE JUICY QUOTATIONS, and we can ignore all the rest.

| 0 | 3 | You now need to refer only to **Source B**, 'The Best Sewing-Machine'. |

How does the writer use language to describe the role of women? **[12 marks]**

Source B

The following article from *Punch*, titled 'The Best Sewing-Machine', is from 1859. The writer explains what qualities he admires in women.

1 The very best Sewing-Machine a man can have is a Wife. It is one that requires but a kind word to set it in motion, rarely gets out of repair, makes but little noise, is seldom the cause of dust, and, once in motion, will go on uninterruptedly for hours, without the slightest trimming, or the smallest personal supervision being necessary. It will

5 make shirts, darn stockings, sew on buttons, mark pocket handkerchiefs, cut out pinafores, and manufacture children's frocks out of any old thing you may give it; and this it will do behind your back just as well as before your face. In fact, you may leave the house for days, and it will go on working just the same. If it does get out of order a little, from being overworked, it mends itself by being left alone for a short time,

10 after which it returns to its sewing with greater vigour than ever. Of course, sewing machines vary a great deal. Some are much quicker than others. It depends in a vast measure upon the particular pattern you select. If you are fortunate in picking out the choicest pattern of a Wife—one, for instance, that sings whilst working, and seems to be never so happy as when the husband's linen is in hand—the Sewing-Machine

15 may be pronounced perfect of its kind; so much so, that there is no make-shift in the world that can possibly replace it, either for love or money. In short, no gentleman's establishment is complete without one of these Sewing-Machines in the house!

Right, so we're looking for THREE JUICY QUOTATIONS about the role of women. I have highlighted a few options in the text but the ones I'm going to go for are:

- *'The very best Sewing-Machine a man can have is a Wife.'* – metaphor, dehumanising women, objectifying them
- *'…darn stockings, sew on buttons…'* – listing duties, sibilance, women expected to be submissive
- *'no gentleman's establishment is complete without one of these Sewing-Machines in the house!'* – exclamation mark, 'sewing machines' contrast with 'gentleman'. This time I will refer to sewing machines as chremamorphism, instead of saying metaphor.

Right, let's put that into three paragraphs:

Firstly, the writer uses language to describe the domestic role of women: 'The very best Sewing-Machine a man can have is a Wife.' Here, the metaphor comparing the wife to a sewing machine reveals the way the woman is objectified and dehumanised. Just like a sewing machine stitches clothes, a woman's role seems to be to keep the family together. The superlative 'best' almost creates a competition amongst women, as if the wives are being ranked according to their domestic performance.

Also, the writer uses linguistic devices to describe how important household chores are in the role of women: 'darn stockings, sew on buttons…'. Here, the use of a long list illustrates the variety of duties that women are expected to carry out but also highlights how endless and never-ending these expectations are. The sibilance within this list subtly conveys the soft and submissive traits that men admire in women, reinforcing the expectation for them to 'go on uninterruptedly' for hours without complaining.

Furthermore, the writer uses language to describe the role of women as being defined as one of service to men: 'no gentleman's establishment is complete without one of these Sewing-Machines in the house!' Here, the use of chremamorphism portrays that a woman's function is to work like a machine in the home, without any feelings or emotions. The noun 'gentleman' is particularly interesting because it contrasts to the description of the sewing machine, cementing the imbalance of power and status between men and women. The exclamation mark reinforces how passionately men believe that women are subservient to men and only exist to benefit them.

So, if we break that down, I have:

1. Written a point that answers the question, using words from the question.
2. Selected a juicy quotation – not too long, not too short.
3. Identified a language device and analysed the effect, linking back to the question.
4. Zoomed in to an interesting word.
5. Zoomed in to a punctuation mark.

We're on a roll! On to Question 4…

Section A – QUESTION 4
16 marks, 20 minutes, 4 paragraphs

You made it to the big Question 4, people. I'm proud of you.

Paper 2, Question 4 looks like this:

| 0 | 4 | For this question, you need to refer to the **whole of Source A**, together with the **whole of Source B**. |

Compare how the writers convey their different attitudes towards women. **[16 marks]**

People often think that this question is the same as Question 2 – the summary of similarities or differences – but it really isn't. This time, you are focusing on what the WRITER thinks and feels about an issue.

Look at this example quotation from another source:

'Children who watch too much television are like untamed hippos.'

Now look at this response:

This shows that children are lazy and watch too much television.

This answer is not about the writer. What does the WRITER think about these children? Does he think they are to blame? No! He is actually blaming the parents.

But HOW DO I KNOW?

Well, this is where the WRITER'S METHODS come in again. What tells me that he thinks the parents are responsible?

- The simile *'like untamed hippos'* shows the writer is critical of how these children have turned out.
- The adjective *'untamed'* shows that he thinks the parents have not been successful in teaching and educating their child in basic manners.
- The phrase *'too much'* proves he feels this amount of television is excessive and therefore detrimental to the child.
- And all of this makes the parent responsible for the failures of the children.

That is basically what we need to try and do, but with these sources.

We will first do it for **Source A**, and then COMPARE it to **Source B**.

Let's remind ourselves what our question was again:

Compare how the writers convey their different attitudes towards women.

From the FIRST HALF of **Source A**, the quotation I will use is:

'How can we shatter these perceptions so that one day…?'

What does the writer think about women? She clearly feels that they are worth more than the way society perceives them and passionately wants to make a change.

So, let's put that into a paragraph:

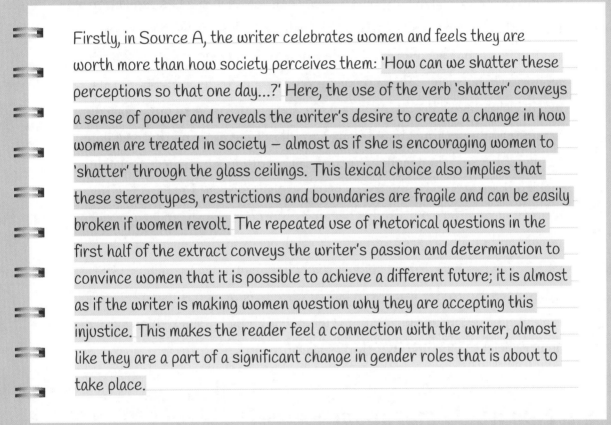

Firstly, in Source A, the writer celebrates women and feels they are worth more than how society perceives them: 'How can we shatter these perceptions so that one day…?' Here, the use of the verb 'shatter' conveys a sense of power and reveals the writer's desire to create a change in how women are treated in society — almost as if she is encouraging women to 'shatter' through the glass ceilings. This lexical choice also implies that these stereotypes, restrictions and boundaries are fragile and can be easily broken if women revolt. The repeated use of rhetorical questions in the first half of the extract conveys the writer's passion and determination to convince women that it is possible to achieve a different future; it is almost as if the writer is making women question why they are accepting this injustice. This makes the reader feel a connection with the writer, almost like they are a part of a significant change in gender roles that is about to take place.

Done. Got some language analysis in there…
Now time to compare.

The quotation I will use from the FIRST PART of **Source B** is:

'If it does get out of order a little,... it mends itself'

So, I'm going to say this writer is very different in his attitude towards women.
He barely sees them as human beings.

Let's put that into a paragraph:

However, in Source B, the writer mocks and ridicules women: 'If it does get out of order a little,... it mends itself'. Here, the conditional clause presents advice to other men about how to keep their wives in the best condition in different scenarios. The pronoun 'it' reveals a lack of respect as the writer clearly feels that his wife is not only unequal to him but not even classified as human in his view. The long complex sentences used throughout this extract also reveal his disregard for the long hours women put into their domestic duties; rather than taking care of her, he explains that she has to 'mend' herself. To a modern reader, this attitude seems unreasonable, making them feel quite shocked by such explicit sexism. Perhaps the two writers have differing attitudes because Source A is written by a modern female author, and therefore holds more progressive views around gender equality; she is delivering a speech to challenge and change minds. On the other hand, Source B is written by a Victorian man who is using the article to protect the status quo, at a time when traditional gender roles were seen as beneficial to men and therefore society.

Done. And then we do that again for paragraphs 3 and 4 with the SECOND HALF of the extracts.

So, if we break that down, I have:

1. Written a point that answers the question, using words from the question, talking about the WRITER'S attitude.
2. Selected a juicy quotation – not too long, not too short.
3. Identified a language device and analysed the effect, linking back to the writer's attitude.
4. Analysed a structural technique to support what I'm saying about how the writer feels.
5. Zoomed in to an interesting word.
6. Explained the effects on the reader.
7. Compared the two sources and explained WHY they have different/similar views.

That's it...

You have nearly finished all of Language Paper 2.

Because this question is worth so many marks, I think it's good to get lots of practice in. So, now try and write two more paragraphs, following the same structure, using quotations from the second half of the sources.

And then... just one more question to go!

TOP TIP!

Zoom out to think about the FORMS of the sources (e.g. if one is a diary... and the other is an article) and the PERSPECTIVES (e.g. if one is written by an adult... and the other is written by a child) to help you in your comparison.

Section B – QUESTION 5 (The WRITING Section)
40 marks, 45 minutes, 1.5–2 pages

The writing section in Paper 2 is different to the writing section in Paper 1. In this paper, you DON'T have a choice of questions. They will give you one question and you HAVE to answer it.

However, the mark scheme is the same – you still have to include all those ingredients we discussed in Paper 1:

- Sophisticated vocabulary
- Language devices
- Different sentence starters
- Long and short sentences
- A range of sophisticated punctuation
- Long and short paragraphs, including a one-line paragraph
- Technical accuracy

TOP TIP!

Just like I said in Paper 1, I would suggest starting with Question 5 first in the exam, and THEN moving on to Questions 1, 2, 3 and 4! Try it out and see if it works for you.

You won't be writing a DESCRIPTION or a STORY in this paper. Instead, you will be doing TRANSACTIONAL writing.

Transactional writing is when you are writing to communicate with someone.

So, you could be asked to write:

- A letter
- A speech
- An article
- A leaflet

If you're writing a letter to someone, or an article, you're obviously not going to just write a beautiful description of the clouds, because that would be really weird.

So, you will be writing to:

- Persuade them
- Advise them
- Argue with them
- Explain something to them

I truly believe this is a life skill…

Transactional writing is something that every human being should know how to do. I spend most of my life writing complaint letters and persuading people to give me a refund… and I always get my money back. So, I strongly suggest you pay attention.

The question will look something like this:

> | 0 | 5 | 'Mobile phones should be banned for all teenagers.'
>
> Write a letter to your local MP in which you argue your point of view on this statement.
>
> (24 marks for content and organisation; 16 marks for technical accuracy) **[40 marks]**

Okay… so where do we begin?

The first thing you need to do is highlight key information in the question. WHAT are you writing and WHO are you writing to? And WHAT are you writing about?

For more on this, see my video:

| 0 | 5 | 'Mobile phones should be banned for all teenagers.'

Write a letter to your local MP in which you argue your point of view on this statement.

(24 marks for content and organisation;
16 marks for technical accuracy)

[40 marks]

Don't skip this step – it literally takes about 5 seconds to do but ensures you don't make any silly mistakes.

For Step 2, you need to figure out your STANCE. What side are you on? Do you agree that mobile phones should be banned for teenagers or not?

You do NOT want to show both sides of the argument: 'I think a little bit yes… but I understand why someone might say no.' How can you win an argument if you show both sides? The only time you bring in the other side is if you are explaining why it is WRONG.

I like to plan by drawing a small, rough table with all the possible arguments I can think of, and then choose the side with the THREE best points.

TOP TIP!

Please note: YOU DO NOT HAVE TO WRITE THE TRUTH. No one cares how you really feel. This is not an honesty exam. You choose whatever side you can argue best in the exam.

YES – BAN MOBILE PHONES	NO – DON'T BAN MOBILE PHONES
Encourages bullying – dangerous – bad for mental health	Safety – you can communicate with parents on your way home from school
Distracts from education	Mental health – helps you to stay in touch with friends during holidays
Dangerous – exposes you to strangers	Helps with education – can do online research, use calculator, etc.
Bad for spelling and education – autocorrect, young people write using text language	
Safety – can get stolen/robbed	

Hmm… this is interesting. Both sides seem quite strong. I want to pick THREE points that are quite DIFFERENT to each other and are not repeating each other… so even though I have MORE points for banning mobile phones, I'm actually going to go for NO – DON'T BAN MOBILE PHONES.

Now that I have planned my points, I'm ready to start writing my letter.

This is a FORMAL letter, so...

You don't need to write an address at the top and all that stuff like you did in primary school. But obviously, you want to be taken seriously, so you can't start with 'HEY MATE! Yo! Wagwan!' (You think I'm joking... trust me, I have seen some shocking formal letters in my time.)

Here are some options for starting your letter:

- *Dear Mr _____,*

    This is nice... it's formal. If you know the local MP's name or it has been stated in the question, you can directly address him or her.

    But if you want to be more sophisticated, you could say something like this:

- *Dear Sir/Madam,*

    I quite like this, particularly if they haven't specified the name of who you are writing to in the question.

    And then you have my personal favourite:

- *To Whom It May Concern,*

    I learnt this when I was young and I used to watch my dad write letters. I really love it – I think it seems so sophisticated. REMEMBER – each word needs a capital letter because it's replacing someone's name.

Now, from there, you need to write an introduction...

Imagine receiving a letter in the post and it says, 'TO MEHREEN MOBILE PHONES SHOULD BE BANNED BECAUSE...'. I'd be like... who are you? Why are you writing to me?

So, you want to include those details in the introduction:

1 What is the issue?
2 Who are you and why do you care?
    (Remember, this doesn't have to be the truth. You can pretend to be whoever you want, e.g. 'As a mother of two teenage girls, I have personally seen the negative impact of mobile phones...').
3 And lastly, what is your stance – what side are you on – and what do you hope to achieve by the end of the letter?

It will look something like this:

> To Whom It May Concern,
> I am writing to you regarding the pressing issue of mobile phone use amongst British teenagers. As a young person myself, I have experienced the benefits of using mobile devices first-hand; I strongly believe that it is crucial for every young person to own a mobile phone and, by the end of this letter, I hope you understand and appreciate my reasons why.

Right, so let's move on...

Now it's time to bring in our actual points that we had planned in the table earlier.

Each point will make something called a BODY PARAGRAPH. So, the introduction is like the head, and now your three body paragraphs will make the main BODY of your letter.

The body paragraph starts with a TOPIC SENTENCE. That is a sentence which summarises what point you're going to be talking about in that paragraph.

So, it looks like this:

Firstly, from a safety perspective, mobile phones should not be banned for teenagers because they can help you to communicate with adults in emergencies.

Now, you need some EVIDENCE to back yourself up. Imagine your parent/guardian telling you that you can't go to a party, and they just say, 'YOU CAN'T GO BECAUSE I SAID SO.' You won't be happy with their decision, will you? But if they said… 'YOU CAN'T GO TO THE PARTY BECAUSE LAST YEAR, 26% OF TEENAGERS WHO WENT TO THAT PARTY FAILED THEIR EXAMS'… you'd be more likely to listen. By giving evidence, you gain credibility and people will trust you more because they assume you know what you're talking about.

These are the three types of evidence you can use:

1 **A statistic.** THIS DOES NOT HAVE TO BE TRUE. No one is expecting you to be an expert on whatever topic they give to you and know real statistics off the top of your head. This isn't a general knowledge quiz. Just make it SOUND realistic. So don't be like '100% OF PEOPLE DIED FROM SMOKING LAST YEAR.' A good statistic looks like this:

Firstly, from a safety perspective, mobile phones should not be banned for teenagers because they can help you to communicate with adults in emergencies. Recent research conducted by the Metropolitan Police revealed that a startling 67% of young people who were attacked last year did not own a mobile phone, hence were unable to call for help.

2 **A quotation from a reliable source.** Pretend someone clever like a professor or a doctor backs up your argument, and give a short quotation from them. For example:

Moreover, from a mental health point of view, mobile phones should not be banned because they help teenagers stay in touch with their friends. Professor Anuja Smith from Cambridge University declared, 'The best way to keep young people feeling positive – especially during holidays – is to ensure they are connected with their peers.'

3 **An anecdote/a pretend famous story.** For example:

Furthermore – if you consider academic progress – mobile phones should not be banned because they can help teenagers with their education. Surely, we haven't forgotten the renowned tale of Krish Gupta – the 14-year-old boy who refused to go to school, and still got all Grade 9s in his GCSEs, simply by revising on his mobile device? His story should have taught us all how powerful this tool can be, when used correctly.

TOP TIP!

Notice how each paragraph starts with a connective (Firstly, Moreover, Furthermore) so the structure of the argument is clear and easy to follow!

Right... we're getting there.

Now, you can't finish a paragraph on evidence...

You need to EXPLAIN FURTHER. What's your point? What do you want us to learn from this evidence? Try to use LANGUAGE DEVICES in this bit. And remember, it should all link back to that topic sentence.

Let me give you an example:

> Firstly, from a safety perspective, mobile phones should not be banned for teenagers because they can help them to communicate with adults in emergencies. Recent research conducted by the Metropolitan Police revealed that a startling 67% of young people who were attacked last year did not own a mobile phone, hence were unable to call for help. By taking away this life-saving technology from our children, we are putting their lives at risk. The world is becoming a dungeon of danger, and we should be doing everything in our power to protect teenagers – not leaving them helpless. Imagine not being able to call your parents to let them know you're running late on your way home from school, or not being able to contact the police if you find yourself in a threatening situation. Does this seem right? Of course not. Banning mobile phones could have detrimental consequences, and the blood would be on your hands.

If you're aiming for a higher level, you can also include these two persuasive techniques in your EXPLAIN FURTHER bits:

1 **Dismiss the counterargument.** Say what the other person might be thinking, and then tell them why they're wrong.

2 **Flattery.** Make the person feel good so they're more likely to listen to you.

The end result will be something like this:

> Moreover, from a mental health point of view, mobile phones should not be banned because they help teenagers stay in touch with their friends. Professor Anuja Smith from Cambridge University declared, 'The best way to keep young people feeling positive – especially during holidays – is to ensure they are connected with their friends.' I understand that some people may think social media actually has a negative impact on teenagers (particularly because of cyber bullying), however, this is completely incorrect and inaccurate because bullying has been happening for decades, even before mobile phones were invented. There will be a mixture of kind and horrible kids, regardless of whether mobile phones exist or not. If they can't bully via mobile phones, they will turn up to your house instead... and that's even more dangerous! We must help our children to maintain a healthy and happy social life, and I know someone as intelligent and knowledgeable as you will be able to see that a healthy social life will inevitably lead to healthier young people.

And finally, it's time for the ending of the letter:

The ending is short and simple. It basically sums up your arguments and gives a final 'I hope you will do the right thing' sort of message. Something like this:

> Keeping all of this in mind, I am positive that you now understand that allowing teenagers to have mobile phones is the key to a happier, safer, more educated society. I hope, and believe, that we can all work together to do the right thing.
>
> Yours faithfully,
> Mehreen Baig

(DON'T FORGET THE COMMA!)

TOP TIP!

You put 'faithfully' at the end if you DID NOT put the person's name at the top. If you put their name, it would be 'Yours sincerely,'. That's the rule.

62

I know that's a lot of information, but...

That's everything you need to know about writing a persuasive letter.

The final product should look something like this:

To Whom It May Concern,

I am writing to you regarding the pressing issue of mobile phone use amongst British teenagers. As a young person myself, I have experienced the benefits of using mobile devices first-hand; I strongly believe that it is crucial for every young person to own a mobile phone and, by the end of this letter, I hope you understand and appreciate my reasons why.

Firstly, from a safety perspective, mobile phones should not be banned for teenagers because they can help you to communicate with adults in emergencies. Recent research conducted by the Metropolitan Police revealed that a startling 67% of young people who were attacked last year did not own a mobile phone, hence were unable to call for help. By taking away this life-saving technology from our children, we are putting their lives at risk. The world is becoming a dungeon of danger, and we should be doing everything in our power to protect teenagers – not leaving them helpless. Imagine not being able to call your parents to let them know you're running late on your way home from school, or not being able to contact the police if you find yourself in a threatening situation. Does this seem right? Of course not. Banning mobile phones could have detrimental consequences, and the blood would be on your hands.

Moreover, from a mental health point of view, mobile phones should not be banned because they help teenagers stay in touch with their friends. Professor Anuja Smith from Cambridge University declared, 'The best way to keep young people feeling positive – especially during holidays – is to ensure they are connected with their friends.' I understand that some people may think social media actually has a negative impact on teenagers (particularly because of cyber bullying), however, this is completely incorrect and inaccurate because bullying has been happening for decades, even before mobile phones were invented. There will be a mixture of kind and horrible kids regardless of whether mobile phones exist or not. If they can't bully via mobile phones, they will turn up to your house instead... and that's even more dangerous! We must help our children to maintain a healthy and happy social life, and I know someone as intelligent and knowledgeable as you will be able to see that a healthy social life will inevitably lead to healthier young people.

Furthermore – if you consider academic progress – mobile phones should not be banned because they can help teenagers with their education. Surely, we haven't forgotten the renowned tale of Krish Gupta – the 14-year-old boy who refused to go to school, and still got all Grade 9s in his GCSEs, simply by revising on his mobile device? His story should have taught us all how powerful this tool can be, when used correctly. Not only do mobile phones give you access to basic educational support like calculators and spellcheck, but they also enable you to download educational apps that can help you to learn at your own pace, in an engaging and accessible way! Whether it's research or revision, the benefits mobile phones bring when it comes to education cannot be disregarded.

Keeping all of this in mind, I am positive that you now understand that allowing teenagers to have mobile phones is the key to a happier, safer, more educated society. I hope, and I believe, that we can all work together to do the right thing.

Yours faithfully,

Mehreen Baig

How are you feeling? I know that's a lot of information... but that's ALL the hard bit done. If you were asked to write in a different form in your exam – like a speech – the body paragraphs would stay the same.

The only thing that would change is your opening and your ending.

So, how do you start a speech?

We want to avoid starting speeches like, 'HELLO, MY NAME IS MEHREEN AND TODAY I WILL TALK TO YOU ABOUT BANNING MOBILE PHONES.' Because that is sooo boring. Imagine if Martin Luther King did that. He wouldn't.

So, we want your opening to be as imaginative, and shocking, and unique as possible. You want to stand out from all the 'HELLO, MY NAME IS MEHREEN' students.

For more on this, see my video:

My FOUR favourite ways to start a speech are:

1 Start with three one-word sentences as a one-line paragraph (like I suggested in Paper 1 – do you remember?). Something like:

> Knowledge. Protection. Power.

It's dramatic. It's interesting. It's different. It will capture the attention of the examiner.

2 Start with a shocking statistic:

> By the time I finish reading this speech, 2.6 million calls will be made to the emergency services.

3 Start with a rhetorical question:

> Have you ever wondered what it's like to be stuck in a dangerous situation, with no way of contacting someone for help?

4 And lastly, my favourite. Start with an *'Imagine this:'*. This gives you the chance to be really creative and descriptive, before getting into the actual persuasive speech. Something like this:

> Imagine this: You're walking down an isolated alleyway on a wintry night. You are engulfed in deep darkness. You are alone. Except... are you? You hear footsteps behind you, approaching softly and slowly at first, before speeding up. Frantically, you reach into your pocket to contact someone for help – for someone to save you. But your pocket is empty. Why?

> Because mobile phones have been banned for teenagers.

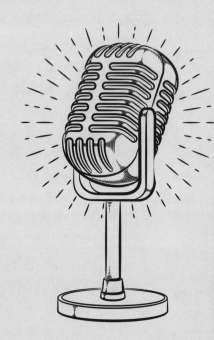

After that, you explain who you are and what your stance is clearly, just as you did in your letter. And then you insert your three body paragraphs.

Now obviously, we can't end a speech, *'Yours faithfully,'*... so you can just end it with the 'I hope you do the right thing' conclusion paragraph. BUT, if you're aiming for the highest level, why not see if you can make your speech cyclical, by referring back to your opening?

Something like this:

> We must ensure no child is ever left exposed in an isolated alleyway with no way to call for help. We must ensure no child ever feels alone. We must not ban mobile phones.

So… we now know how to:

- Write a persuasive letter, AND
- A persuasive speech.

But what if you're asked to write an article or a leaflet?

It's basically the same thing, except YOU NEED A HEADLINE. Try to make this catchy, so use alliteration or a pun – for example:

- Ban-droid!
- No More Cell-fies!
- Cell Out!
- No-bile Phones for Teenagers!

I had way too much fun thinking of those! Anyway, if you can't think of a pun on the day, it really doesn't matter. Alliteration or even a rhetorical question will do the job. For example:

- Cutting the Cord!
- Should Monstrous Mobiles Be Banned?

And then the rest of the article is similar to the structure of the speech – just slightly less chatty and conversational.

Right… you have all the knowledge you need. Why don't you pick a topic from the list below and try writing a letter about it, then turn it into a speech, and then an article. You will feel SO much better once you've given it a go yourself.

- 'Online learning is more effective than traditional classroom learning.'
- 'The voting age should be lowered to 16.'
- 'There should be no more school uniforms.'
- 'Footballers should be paid more than teachers.' (Umm… NO.)

And that's all folks! English Language has come to an end.

Now go and have a well-deserved rest… until we meet again for Literature xx

65

LITERATURE PAPER 1 – OVERVIEW

> I LOVE LITERATURE! And I promise, by the end of this guide, you will love it too.

Paper 1 is called **Shakespeare and the 19th-century novel**.
So, there are two sections – **Section A** (Shakespeare) and **Section B** (19th-century novel).

Your Shakespeare text will be one of the following:

- *Macbeth*
- *Romeo and Juliet*
- *The Tempest*
- *The Merchant of Venice*
- *Much Ado About Nothing*
- *Julius Caesar*

Your 19th-century text will be one of the following:

- *The Strange Case of Dr Jekyll and Mr Hyde*
- *A Christmas Carol*
- *Great Expectations*
- *Jane Eyre*
- *Frankenstein*
- *Pride and Prejudice*
- *The Sign of Four*

You will read the texts in class with your teacher, and I recommend you read them over and over again at home as many times as you can before the real exam. If you're in **Year 10**, read your texts once every THREE months to keep them fresh in your head. If you're in **Year 11** and there isn't long left until your exams, try to read a couple of chapters for half an hour EVERY night before bed instead of going on TikTok.

Trust me – it will make a massive difference.

Read the texts over and over again at home.

Some key things you need to know are:

- You will answer one question from Section A and one question from Section B. THERE IS NO CHOICE OF QUESTION.

- The paper is 1 hour 45 minutes long.

- Both sections are equally weighted – the essays are worth 30 marks each. So, you spend around 50 minutes on each section, and spend **5 minutes** planning and checking your work.

- **Section A** (Shakespeare) has an ADDITIONAL 4 MARKS available for spelling, punctuation and grammar. 4 marks can make a big difference – so pay attention to your writing!

- You will be given an extract for both questions.

- You will be asked to start your essays focusing on the extracts and then write about other parts of both texts.

- You are not allowed to take any books into the exam with you, so you have to know the texts inside out, including key quotations.

- For each question, you should aim to write THREE to FOUR paragraphs. Preferably two about the extract, and one or two about elsewhere in the text.

- Try to cover the beginning, middle and end of the text if possible – so if the extract is from the MIDDLE of the text, your other evidence should be from the BEGINNING and the END.

Now, this bit is really important...

Every PARAGRAPH you write in your Literature exams will follow this BASIC STRUCTURE:

1. A point that answers the question using key words from the question

2. Evidence

3. Analysis of language and structure, linking back to the point/question

4. Context, writer's intention, effect on audience/reader

> *You are not allowed to take any books into the exam with you, so you have to know the texts inside out.*

Keep this structure in your mind.

In the next few sections, I'm going to show you how to do each of these steps.

I'll add a new skill in every section, so by the end of it, you know how to write TOP LEVEL paragraphs.

Section A – SHAKESPEARE

Do not hate on Shakespeare. He INVENTED words we use today like 'swagger'. He was rapping poetry to the beat before Dave was even born. Shakespeare is the OG (the Original Genius).

Your Shakespeare question will look like this:

| 0 | 1 | Read the following extract from Act 1 Scene 1 of *Romeo and Juliet* and then answer the question that follows.

At this point in the play, Tybalt joins in the fight between the servants.

Starting with this moment in the play, explore how Shakespeare presents Tybalt as an aggressive character.

Write about:
- how Shakespeare presents Tybalt in this extract
- how Shakespeare presents Tybalt as an aggressive character in the play as a whole.

[30 marks] AO4 [4 marks]

You should always READ THE QUESTION first because it helps you to understand what's going on in the extract and tells you what you are looking for.

Don't worry if *Romeo and Juliet* isn't your Shakespeare text – you can still give this a go and use it as practice. Tybalt is Juliet's cousin. He wants to fight anyone who is from Romeo's family (the Montagues). Romeo's lovely cousin, Benvolio, tries to stop a fight that's broken out in public between both sides, but Tybalt isn't having it…

Let's give the extract a read:

TYBALT
What, art thou drawn among these heartless hinds?
Turn thee, Benvolio, look upon thy death.
BENVOLIO
I do but keep the peace. Put up thy sword,
Or manage it to part these men with me.
TYBALT
5   What, drawn and talk of peace? I hate the word.
As I hate hell, all Montagues, and thee.
Have at thee, coward! [They fight.]

> ### TOP TIP!
>
> The extract in the real exam will be a bit longer than this – but don't worry! You will approach it in exactly the same way.

Next, we need to start planning and annotating...

I'm going to highlight any evidence in the extract that makes Tybalt seem aggressive, and also label any important words, language devices or punctuation marks that I spot. I will ignore all the irrelevant bits that aren't about Tybalt being aggressive.

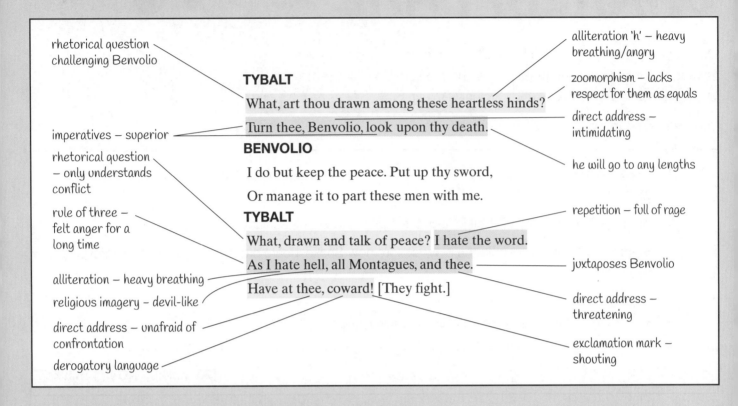

rhetorical question challenging Benvolio

imperatives – superior

rhetorical question – only understands conflict

rule of three – felt anger for a long time

alliteration – heavy breathing

religious imagery – devil-like

direct address – unafraid of confrontation

derogatory language

alliteration 'h' – heavy breathing/angry

zoomorphism – lacks respect for them as equals

direct address – intimidating

he will go to any lengths

repetition – full of rage

juxtaposes Benvolio

direct address – threatening

exclamation mark – shouting

TYBALT

What, art thou drawn among these heartless hinds?
Turn thee, Benvolio, look upon thy death.

BENVOLIO

I do but keep the peace. Put up thy sword,
Or manage it to part these men with me.

TYBALT

What, drawn and talk of peace? I hate the word.
As I hate hell, all Montagues, and thee.
Have at thee, coward! [They fight.]

There is SO much in there!

It is clear Tybalt is TRYING to pick a fight with Benvolio, even though Benvolio doesn't want it. I need to put that into a good POINT SENTENCE using key words from the question to start my essay off.

> Starting with this moment in the play, explore how Shakespeare presents Tybalt as an aggressive character.

Firstly, Shakespeare presents Tybalt as an aggressive character.

Is this a good point sentence? NO. I've basically just repeated the question – not answered it. It's like someone saying, 'Why is Mehreen a good teacher?' and you answer 'Firstly, Mehreen is a good teacher.' So, let's try that again:

Firstly, in this extract, Shakespeare presents Tybalt as an aggressive character because he deliberately instigates fights.

Notice a couple of things I have done there. Firstly, I clearly signposted that I was talking about the extract, which makes it really easy for the examiner to see that I have covered both THE EXTRACT and ELSEWHERE IN THE PLAY in my essay. Secondly, I wrote a BECAUSE and gave a reason why Tybalt is aggressive.

Let's try that again…

This time let's use *The Merchant of Venice*. Shylock is a Jewish businessman who believes he has been discriminated against. In this scene, he talks about how unfairly he has been treated, as if he's not even a human being.

Here's the question:

---

0 1 Read the following extract from Act 3 Scene 1 of *The Merchant of Venice* and then answer the question that follows.

At this point in the play, Shylock is talking to Salerio about how he has been treated.

> **SALERIO**
> Why, I am sure, if he forfeit, thou wilt not take his flesh.
> What's that good for?
>
> **SHYLOCK**
> To bait fish withal. If it will feed nothing else, it will feed my revenge. He hath disgraced me, and hindered me half a million,
> 5 laughed at my losses, mocked at my gains, scorned my nation, thwarted my bargains, cooled my friends, heated mine enemies, and what's the reason? I am a Jew. Hath not a Jew eyes? Hath not a Jew hands, organs, dimensions, senses, affections, passions? Fed with the same food, hurt with the same weapons, subject to
> 10 the same diseases, healed by the same means, warmed and cooled by the same winter and summer, as a Christian is? If you prick us, do we not bleed? If you tickle us, do we not laugh? If you poison us, do we not die? And if you wrong us, shall we not revenge? If we are like you in the rest, we will resemble you in that. If a Jew
> 15 wrong a Christian, what is his humility? Revenge. If a Christian wrong a Jew, what should his sufferance be by Christian example? Why, revenge. The villainy you teach me I will execute, and it shall go hard but I will better the instruction.

Starting with this moment in the play, explore how Shakespeare presents Shylock as a victim.

Write about:

- how Shakespeare presents Shylock in this extract
- how Shakespeare presents Shylock as a victim in the play as a whole.

[30 marks] AO4 [4 marks]

So again, the first thing we do is HIGHLIGHT and LABEL THE EXTRACT with anything that makes Shylock seem like a victim… Try to give it a go yourself, and then have a look at what I found:

SALERIO

Why, I am sure, if he forfeit, thou wilt not take his flesh.
What's that good for?

SHYLOCK

To bait fish withal. If it will feed nothing else, it will feed my
revenge. He hath disgraced me, and hindered me half a million,
laughed at my losses, mocked at my gains, scorned my nation,
thwarted my bargains, cooled my friends, heated mine enemies,
and what's the reason? I am a Jew. Hath not a Jew eyes? Hath
not a Jew hands, organs, dimensions, senses, affections, passions?
Fed with the same food, hurt with the same weapons, subject to
the same diseases, healed by the same means, warmed and cooled
by the same winter and summer, as a Christian is? If you prick us,
do we not bleed? If you tickle us, do we not laugh? If you poison
us, do we not die? And if you wrong us, shall we not revenge? If
we are like you in the rest, we will resemble you in that. If a Jew
wrong a Christian, what is his humility? Revenge. If a Christian
wrong a Jew, what should his sufferance be by Christian
example? Why, revenge. The villainy you teach me I will
execute, and it shall go hard but I will better the instruction.

Annotations (left):
- verbs – humiliated
- alliteration 'l' – people have enjoyed mocking him
- repetition – defined by his religion
- alliteration 'h' – sadness
- visceral imagery – humanises him
- semantic field of pain – hurt
- inclusive pronouns – not just his suffering, his whole community

Annotations (right):
- personification, but this quotation is irrelevant. It doesn't make him seem like a victim. It makes him seem angry
- alliteration 'h' – sighing, sadness
- asyndetic list – been mistreated for a long time
- rhetorical questions – doesn't understand why he has been treated in this way
- asyndetic list – emphasising similarities
- list of conditional questions – sense of unfairness

Poor Shylock. They treat him so badly just because of his religion.

So, let's put that into a point sentence:

> Starting with this moment in the play, explore how Shakespeare presents Shylock as a victim.

Firstly, **in this extract**, Shakespeare presents Shylock as a
victim **because** he faces unjust discrimination.

Have you got the hang of it now?

Shall we try one with Macbeth?

In this scene, Macbeth tells his wife, Lady Macbeth, that he doesn't
want to kill King Duncan. She is absolutely furious.

For more on this,
see my video:

| 0 | 1 | Read the following extract from Act 1 Scene 7 of *Macbeth* and then answer the question that follows.

At this point in the play, Lady Macbeth is persuading her husband to kill the king.

Starting with this moment in the play, explore how Shakespeare presents Lady Macbeth as a
powerful woman.

Write about:
- how Shakespeare presents Lady Macbeth in this extract
- how Shakespeare presents Lady Macbeth as a powerful woman in the play as a whole.

[30 marks] AO4 [4 marks]

alliteration 'w' – cannot understand why he hasn't fulfilled his promise

metaphor – ironic because she's asking him to do a monstrous thing

direct address – accusatory tone

juxtaposition – the lengths she is willing to go to

inclusive pronoun – pretending they are a team

metaphor – using him like a tool to gain power

rhetorical question – challenging him

personal pronoun – selfish

repetition – challenging his masculinity

hyperbole – violent

killing baby is symbolic of destroying innocence

bilabial plosive alliteration – hard and callous

breaks adjacency pairs by asking a question back to his question – mocks his fears

imperative – commanding him

LADY MACBETH

What beast was't, then,

That made you break this enterprise to me?

When you durst do it, then you were a man:

And to be more than what you were, you would

Be so much more the man. Nor time nor place

Did then adhere, and yet you would make both:

They have made themselves, and that their fitness now

Does unmake you. I have given suck, and know

How tender 'tis to love the babe that milks me:

I would, while it was smiling in my face,

Have plucked my nipple from his boneless gums,

And dashed the brains out, had I so sworn as you

Have done to this.

MACBETH

If we should fail?

LADY MACBETH

We fail?

But screw your courage to the sticking place

And we'll not fail.

Starting with this moment in the play, explore how Shakespeare presents Lady Macbeth as a powerful woman.

Firstly, **in this extract,** Shakespeare presents Lady Macbeth as a powerful woman **due** to the way she controls her husband's actions, despite him being a courageous soldier.

I think you get the picture now.

So, what's our next step after we have written a point?

1 A point that answers the question using words from the question ✓

2 Evidence

3 Analysis of language and structure, linking back to the point/question

4 Context, writer's intention, effect on audience/reader

TOP TIP!

Adjacency pairs are an expected pattern of conversation between two people. For example, if I ask you a question, I expect you to respond with an answer. If you respond to a question with a question, you're BREAKING adjacency pairs.

The next step is to bring in EVIDENCE. We need to select a QUOTATION that proves our point is TRUE.

There will be lots of quotations in the extract that will answer the question and prove your point, but you need to pick the JUICIEST one. That means the one with the MOST amount of language devices, interesting words and punctuation that you can zoom in to and talk about. For example, I could use the following quotation to show Lady Macbeth's power:

'And to be more than what you were, you would/ Be so much more the man.'

But after I've spoken about the word 'man' in my explanation, I won't have anything else to say. So instead, I'm going to use this:

Firstly, in this extract, Shakespeare presents Lady Macbeth as a powerful woman due to the way she controls her husband's actions, despite him being a courageous soldier. This is evident when Macbeth explains that he does not want to kill the king, and she shows her displeasure by asking, 'What beast was't, then,/ That made you break this enterprise to me?'

So, now we have...

1 A point that answers the question using words from the question ✓
2 Evidence ✓

What's next?

Now we have to EXPLAIN what the quotation shows, and HOW it proves our point:

Firstly, in this extract, Shakespeare presents Lady Macbeth as a powerful woman due to the way she controls her husband's actions, despite him being a courageous soldier. This is evident when Macbeth explains that he does not want to kill the king, and she shows her displeasure by asking, 'What beast was 't, then,/ That made you break this enterprise to me?' Here, the rhetorical question displays how Lady Macbeth is boldly challenging her husband's decision, highlighting her power within this relationship; her incredulity is further reinforced through the alliteration of 'w', as though she cannot understand why Macbeth does not want to fulfil his 'enterprise' to her by committing regicide. The fact that Lady Macbeth directly addresses her husband when she says 'you' creates an accusatory tone, as though she blames the eponymous hero for being too weak, and her selfish nature is cemented through the personal pronoun 'me', as it becomes clear she wants Macbeth to commit this act for her own personal gain, so she can become even more powerful. Shakespeare's use of the metaphor 'beast' is ironic, as it is Lady Macbeth who is asking her husband to do a 'beastly' and monstrous thing, manipulating him and taking advantage of the power she has over him.

TOP TIP!

Notice how I keep referring back to the word POWER throughout my explanation, to prove I am staying relevant to the question.

TOP TIP!

Try to mention the words 'stage directions', 'aside' and 'soliloquy' in your explanation, where possible. This shows the examiner that you understand this is a PLAY. An aside is when a character is speaking his/her thoughts aloud but other characters are on stage. A soliloquy is the same thing but no one else is on stage.

This time we have...

1 A point that answers the question using words from the question ✓

2 Evidence ✓

3 Analysis of language and structure, linking back to the point/question ✓

The paragraph is looking beautiful, but it isn't finished just yet. We need to round off by EVALUATING – bringing in **context** and **writer's intention**. This means I need to explain what society was like during the time the play was written, and then explain what message Shakespeare was trying to give to the audience.

Here's some Elizabethan/Jacobean context you should know about:

*   Religion – people were very religious. They believed in heaven and hell and that God punished their sins.
*   The role of women – they were expected to be submissive, subservient, pious, and against violence. Society was patriarchal (ruled by men).
*   The role of men – there was a huge emphasis on masculinity. Men were expected to be violent and aggressive, dominating their households.
*   The supernatural/witchcraft – society believed in supernatural forces. King James even wrote a book about witches called *Daemonologie*.
*   The Divine Right of the King – people believed that God had selected the king, therefore going against him was not just a crime, but a religious sin.
*   The Gunpowder Plot – when Shakespeare wrote *Macbeth*, Guy Fawkes had recently tried to commit regicide (kill the king) in the gunpowder plot. So, the threat to the throne was real.
*   The Great Chain of Being – people believed that there was a natural order to everything. If you were a servant, God wanted you to be that way, so you shouldn't try to jump the queue.

The context we add to the end of each paragraph shouldn't be random – it should be RELEVANT to the paragraph you are writing. So, in this Lady Macbeth paragraph, I can't bring in 'society believed in witchcraft', because it wouldn't link to what I'm talking about.

So instead, I'm going to do this:

Firstly, in this extract, Shakespeare presents Lady Macbeth as a powerful woman due to the way she controls her husband's actions, despite him being a courageous soldier. This is evident when Macbeth explains that he does not want to kill the king, and she shows her displeasure by asking, 'What beast was 't, then,/ That made you break this enterprise to me?' Here, the rhetorical question displays how Lady Macbeth is boldly challenging her husband's decision, highlighting her power within this relationship; her incredulity is further reinforced through the alliteration of 'w', as though she cannot understand why Macbeth does not want to fulfil his 'enterprise' to her by committing regicide. The fact that Lady Macbeth directly addresses her husband when she says 'you' creates an accusatory tone, as though she blames the eponymous hero for being too weak, and her selfish nature is cemented through the personal pronoun 'me', as it becomes clear she wants Macbeth to commit this act for her own personal gain, so she can become even more powerful. Shakespeare's use of the metaphor 'beast' is ironic, as it is Lady Macbeth who is asking her husband to do a 'beastly' and monstrous thing, manipulating him and taking advantage of the power she has over him. Lady Macbeth's behaviour towards her husband would have been very shocking for a Jacobean audience, as women were expected to be submissive towards their husbands, and men were supposed to hold the power within households in the patriarchal system. Hence, by portraying their anachronistic relationship, perhaps Shakespeare was warning the audience against giving women too much power. But the way Shakespeare deliberately intertwines female power with villainy may be disappointing for a modern audience.

Is that looking like a top grade paragraph? Oh yes, it is!

So, we have done:

1. A point that answers the question using words from the question ✓
2. Evidence ✓
3. Analysis of language and structure, linking back to the point/question ✓
4. Context, writer's intention, effect on audience/reader ✓

If that looked quite tricky to do, don't worry...

In the next section, I'll break down how to do the blue bit – the ANALYSIS – in a bit more detail.

> ### TOP TIP!
>
> 'Anachronistic' means something that doesn't belong to that time period. For example, if you are studying *Much Ado About Nothing*, Beatrice is also anachronistic due to her outspoken nature, rejection of traditional matrimony, and the way she challenges the male characters.

Section B – THE 19TH-CENTURY NOVEL

Now that we know what a basic paragraph should look like, I'm going to show you how you can make your EXPLANATIONS – your analysis – longer and more perceptive. YOUR MARKS LIE IN THE ANALYSIS, so the more detailed and interesting you can be in your explanation, the higher the mark you'll get.

In your explanation, you DO NOT WANT TO SAY GENERIC THINGS LIKE, *'This makes it stand out'* or *'This creates tension'* or… wait for it… *'This makes you want to read on'*. What on earth does that even mean? I don't even need to give you an extract or a text for you to write *'This makes you want to read on'*. Your explanations need to be SPECIFIC.

A good analysis should have THREE layers.

Look at your quotation and think:
- What will **ALL** the class say about this quotation?
- What will **HALF** the class say about this quotation?
- What can **ONLY YOU** think of?

So, let's look at this quotation from Dickens' *A Christmas Carol*. It is the opening description of the protagonist, Scrooge, who is a selfish character who doesn't like Christmas, or people, very much.

> *'Hard and sharp as flint, from which no steel had ever struck out generous fire…'*

- **ALL** the class will probably be able to identify that there is a SIMILE in this quotation: *'hard and sharp as flint'*. They may say that, *'This shows Scrooge is an uncaring and stony character who doesn't allow anyone close to him.'*
- **HALF** the class may say something like, *'This shows Scrooge causes pain to others just like a "sharp" stone would do. Also, this chremamorphism may show that Scrooge lacks human compassion and has become almost lifeless as a consequence of his selfishness and greed.'*
- **ONLY YOU** (after reading this revision guide) will say, *'However, perhaps this comparison could demonstrate that Scrooge has the potential to offer joy and warmth to others around him, just like a "flint" is capable of lighting a fire.'*

Now, imagine you are using this quotation to answer a question about Scrooge being presented as an uncaring character. If you were an examiner, what would you say about this paragraph?

> At the beginning of 'A Christmas Carol', Scrooge is presented as an uncaring character due to the emphasis on his cruel nature. This is evident in his initial description where the writer lists all of Scrooge's flaws: 'hard and sharp as flint, from which no steel had ever struck out generous fire'. Here, the use of chremamorphism gives the impression that Scrooge has the potential to spark a feeling of warmth in others, just like a 'flint' is able to light a fire.

This is what I would say:

Things that are done well
- There is a clear point which answers the question.
- A juicy quotation is included.
- A language device is identified.

Things that are NOT done well
- Although a unique interpretation of Scrooge's potential has been highlighted, there is no general understanding of the effect of Scrooge being compared to a stone.
- Context/writer's intention is missing.
- Dickens' name is not mentioned.

Now, take a look at an improved version:

> At the beginning of 'A Christmas Carol', Scrooge is presented as an uncaring character due to the emphasis on his cruel nature. This is evident in his initial description where the writer lists all of Scrooge's flaws: 'hard and sharp as flint, from which no steel had ever struck out generous fire'. Here, the use of the simile gives the impression that Scrooge is an uncaring and stony character who doesn't allow anyone close to him, as he seems to be hardened to any generosity or kindness. It appears Scrooge causes pain to others just like a 'sharp' stone would do. Also, this chremamorphism may show that Scrooge lacks human compassion and has become almost lifeless as a consequence of his selfishness and greed — an idea that foreshadows the corpse that Scrooge will become in Stave Four. In this way, the lack of 'generous fire' can be implying a lack of warmth that Scrooge exhibits, reinforcing his cold and cruel attitude. However, Dickens could have intentionally employed this comparison to convey that Scrooge has the potential to spark a warmth in others, just like a 'flint' is able to light a fire. Perhaps the spark is not just a sign of Scrooge's potential for change but is Dickens using Scrooge as a microcosm for the mercenary nature of Victorian society as a whole — which he hopes, through his readers, he can change too.

TOP TIP!

Did you see what I did there when I mentioned Stave Four? If you're feeling really confident, you can refer to other parts of the text within your extract paragraphs too.

I know that's a lot to take in...

So, let's do it all over again...

Let's try it with a practice exam question on a different text. The more we practise, the better we will get.

Look at this example question on *The Strange Case of Dr Jekyll and Mr Hyde*:

0 1 Read the following extract from Chapter 2 and then answer the question that follows.

In this extract, Mr Hyde is described for the first time.

> 'We have common friends,' said Mr Utterson.
>
> 'Common friends!' echoed Mr Hyde, a little hoarsely. 'Who are they?'
>
> 'Jekyll, for instance,' said the lawyer.
>
> 'He never told you,' cried Mr Hyde, with a flush of anger. 'I did not think you would
> 5 have lied.'
>
> 'Come,' said Mr Utterson, 'that is not fitting language.'
>
> The other snarled aloud into a savage laugh; and the next moment, with extraordinary
> quickness, he had unlocked the door and disappeared into the house. The lawyer stood
> awhile when Mr Hyde had left him, the picture of disquietude. Then he began slowly to
> 10 mount the street, pausing every step or two and putting his hand to his brow like a man
> in mental perplexity. The problem he was thus debating as he walked was one of a class
> that is rarely solved. Mr Hyde was pale and dwarfish; he gave an impression of deformity
> without any nameable malformation, he had a displeasing smile, he had borne himself to
> the lawyer with a sort of murderous mixture of timidity and boldness, and he spoke with a
> 15 husky whispering and somewhat broken voice, – all these were points against him; but not
> all of these together could explain the hitherto unknown disgust, loathing and fear with
> which Mr Utterson regarded him.

Starting with this extract, how does Stevenson present Mr Hyde as a wild and inhuman character?
Write about:

- how Stevenson presents Mr Hyde in this extract
- how Stevenson presents Mr Hyde as a wild and inhuman character in the novel as a whole.

[30 marks]

So, let's go step by step. We want...

1 A point that answers the question using words from the question

2 A juicy quotation

3 Analysis of language and structure, linking back to the point/question

4 Context, writer's intention, effect on audience, linking back to point/question

I need a point:

In this extract, Stevenson presents Mr Hyde as a wild and inhuman character by highlighting how different he is from the other civilised characters.

Next, let's select a JUICY QUOTATION from the extract.

I need one that makes Hyde seem like a wild and inhuman character.

These are the options I have found:

- '... with a flush of anger.' – This makes him seem scary, right? But what would I actually say about it? This shows Mr Hyde has a bad temper... and then what? There is no interesting language device for me to really talk about in detail.

- 'Mr Hyde was pale and dwarfish...' – This is a bit better. 'Pale' has death imagery, so it definitely makes Mr Hyde seem frightening... and 'dwarfish' makes him seem different to other humans. Two interesting adjectives... hmm...

- 'he had a displeasing smile' – A nice oxymoron here. 'Smiles' are supposed to be positive, but his is 'displeasing'. That makes him seem quite sinister and unsettling, like even good things turn bad with him.

- 'murderous mixture of timidity and boldness' – I really like this one. There's alliteration of 'm', which creates an effect of hunger, as if he is a predator ready to devour his prey... we could zoom in to the adjective 'murderous'... and then there's the juxtaposition of 'timidity and boldness' which makes him seem unpredictable.

- '...unknown disgust, loathing and fear with which Mr Utterson regarded him.' – A rule of three here. Mr Utterson is clearly not a fan of Mr Hyde.

- '... snarled aloud into a savage laugh... disappeared into the house.' – This is my favourite one. There is onomatopoeia in 'snarled', and that's also zoomorphism because it's an animal sound. There is sibilance in 'snarled' and 'savage', and an oxymoron in 'savage laugh'... and then I can zoom in to the verb 'disappeared'.

Have a think – which one would you choose to get the most interesting analysis?

Here's the one I chose, with my THREE layers of analysis:

'...snarled aloud into a savage laugh... disappeared into the house.'

- 'snarled' onomatopoeia – dangerous
- 'snarled'/'savage' sibilance – snaky sound, sinister, devious
- 'snarled' zoomorphism – regressed into animalistic behaviour and lost all sense of humanity
- 'savage laugh' oxymoron – unsettling, takes pleasure in other people's pain
- 'snarled' turns into 'savage laugh' – mood quickly escalates, unpredictable
- 'disappeared' verb – almost otherworldly

And finally...

Let's put it into a paragraph, adding context and writer's message at the end:

In this extract, Stevenson presents Mr Hyde as a wild and inhuman character by highlighting how different he is from the other civilised characters. When Utterson tries to confront Hyde, he 'snarled aloud into a savage laugh' and 'disappeared into the house'. Here, the onomatopoeic verb, 'snarled', conveys how wild and dangerous Hyde is. Furthermore, both 'snarled' and 'savage' are linked through sibilance – which mimics the sound of a snake – reflecting Hyde's sinister and devious character. Stevenson also employs zoomorphism in 'snarled', perhaps illustrating how Hyde has almost regressed into animalistic behaviour and lost all sense of humanity. His 'savage laugh' may be seen as oxymoronic, which is unsettling for both Utterson and the reader, as it implies that Hyde takes pleasure in other people's pain. The fact 'snarled' swiftly turns into a 'savage laugh' demonstrates how quickly Hyde's mood escalates, and how wild and unpredictable his behaviour is. At the same time, the verb 'disappeared' reflects how inhuman and almost otherworldly Hyde seems to be, like a magician, who manages to 'hide' from accountability and the judgement of others. Perhaps Stevenson is trying to suggest that the Victorian emphasis on politeness and etiquette almost forced young men like Dr Jekyll into living a dual life. As Mr Hyde represents the side of Dr Jekyll that is outside society's norms and must be kept hidden, Stevenson implies that this wildness becomes worse due to its suppression.

Remember, you have to write two or three more paragraphs, one more on the extract, and the rest on other parts of the novel.

Why don't you use the example paragraph we just wrote and try to write one more paragraph of your own? You could try a generic theme, like power, and choose an extract from your own text. For example, I LOVE the confrontation between Lady Catherine De Bourgh and Elizabeth in *Pride and Prejudice*, where Lady Catherine abuses her power as a wealthy woman to insult Elizabeth; or, if you are studying one of the other texts, you could look at the power of wealth in *The Sign of Four*, or the power of science in *Frankenstein*, or the power of women in *Jane Eyre*. See? It applies to everything!

TOP TIP!

Use words like 'perhaps' and 'could be' in your explanation, to show these are just YOUR INTERPRETATIONS – you didn't go and speak to the writer and find out what they DEFINITELY MEANT. No spoiler here, but as the texts are 19th century, the writers are definitely dead.

I hope you're feeling good...
because you only have Literature Paper 2 to go...

LITERATURE PAPER 2 – OVERVIEW

> Right, guys.
> One more
> (very long but
> super interesting)
> exam paper
> to go.

Literature Paper 2 is called **Modern Texts and Poetry**. There are THREE sections: **Section A** (Modern texts), **Section B** (Poetry Anthology) and **Section C** (Unseen poetry).

Your modern text will be one of the following:

- *An Inspector Calls*
- *Blood Brothers* (musical version)
- *The History Boys* (last exam 2024)
- *DNA*
- *The Curious Incident of the Dog in the Night-Time* (playscript – last exam 2024)
- *A Taste of Honey*
- *Princess & The Hustler* (first teaching 2023)
- *Leave Taking* (first teaching 2023)
- *Lord of the Flies*
- *AQA Anthology: Telling Tales*
- *Animal Farm*
- *Never Let Me Go* (last exam 2024)
- *Anita and Me*
- *Pigeon English*
- *My Name is Leon* (first teaching 2023)

Your poetry cluster will be one of t he following:

- 'Love and Relationships' (15 poems)
- 'Power and Conflict' (15 poems)
- 'Worlds and Lives' (15 poems – first teaching 2023)

Like Paper 1, you will read the texts in class with your teacher, but you need to keep RE-READING them to keep them fresh in your mind.

Some things you need to know about this paper are:

- You will answer **one** question from **Section A**, **one** question from **Section B**, and **two** questions from **Section C**.
- The paper is 2 hours 15 minutes long.
- **Section A** is worth 30 marks + 4 marks for spelling, punctuation and grammar.
- **Section B** is worth 30 marks.
- **Section C** is worth 32 marks (24 marks for the first question and 8 marks for the second question).
- So, each section is sort of worth the same amount of marks, which means you will spend the same amount of time on each section. In total, the paper is worth 96 marks.

Don't worry – let's go through it section by section so you know exactly what to do.

Each section is sort of worth the same amount of marks, which means you will spend the same amount of time on each.

Section A – MODERN TEXTS

The bad news is... you are NOT given an extract in this section. But the good news is... you are given a CHOICE of two questions. The question can be based on a character, theme or setting.

The question will look something like this:

Answer **one** question from this section on your chosen text.

JB Priestley: *An Inspector Calls*

Either

| 0 | 1 | How far does Priestley present the Birling family as self-centred in the play?

Write about:
- one or more of the Birling family
- how far Priestley presents one or more of the Birling family as self-centred.

[30 marks]
AO4 [4 marks]

or

| 0 | 2 | How does Priestley present Sheila as a character who matures over the course of the play?

Write about:
- what Sheila says and does
- how Priestley presents Sheila as a character who matures over the course of the play.

[30 marks]
AO4 [4 marks]

For this question, you should write THREE paragraphs in around 45 minutes. That's not too bad is it? Now, you're not allowed to take your book into your exam with you AND there's no extract... so you have to MEMORISE the JUICIEST quotations. I know a lot of students freak out about that, but it really isn't as scary as it sounds.

In your essay, you want to cover the WHOLE TEXT... so ideally, you want to write a paragraph about the BEGINNING, a paragraph about the MIDDLE and a paragraph about the END. What I like to do is find THREE JUICY quotations for each character (one from near the beginning of the text, one from the middle, and one towards the end) and just memorise those.

Every character has an arc – they all go on some sort of journey throughout the story. They change in some way... they develop in some way. By thinking about their journey in advance, you can save time planning in the exam.

Let's think about Mr Birling in An Inspector Calls...

At the beginning, he's a strong capitalist who only cares about himself and money... in the middle of the play, he pretends to show some sort of remorse about Eva Smith's death... and at the end, he reverts back to his original ways, refusing to take any responsibility for his actions.

In contrast, Sheila – his daughter – is spoilt and superficial at the start of the play, but in the middle, she genuinely feels bad about the part she had to play in Eva Smith's death, and by the end, she completely understands the importance of social responsibility.

I like to draw out the THREE best quotations for every character on REVISION CARDS.

A bit like this:

Sheila

B: Spoilt and superficial:
'Look – Mummy – isn't it a beauty?'

M: Begins to feel empathy for working class and challenges her parents' views:
'But these girls aren't cheap labour – they're people!'

E: Learns the important lesson of accepting responsibility:
'Fire and blood and anguish. And it frightens me the way you talk.'

You can use different colours and make your revision cards nice and pretty... and you can also add some analysis notes if you like.

Like this:

Sheila

B: Spoilt and superficial:
'Look – Mummy – isn't it a beauty?'

Rhetorical question – needs reassurance/excited, values material things. Imperative – desperate for attention. 'Mummy' – childish, immature, dependent.

M: Begins to feel empathy for working class and challenges her parents' views:
'But these girls aren't cheap labour – they're people!'

Conjunction 'But'– disagreeing with parents. Exclamation mark – deeply remorseful and horrified.

E: Learns the important lesson of accepting responsibility:
'Fire and blood and anguish. And it frightens me the way you talk.'

Repeating Inspector's words, usurped his role. Polysyndeton – contrast to earlier fragmented dialogue. Maturity. Direct address – accusatory tone.

Creating a revision card like this for every character will not actually take that long – even if you spent a REALLY long time on it, and REALLY went through EVERY SINGLE QUOTATION before selecting your final three, you'd still be done in a couple of days.

There are characters where this arc will be obvious, like Edward in *Blood Brothers*. Adopted by Mr and Mrs Lyons, he initially prospers in his new family but then struggles to escape his past and is tragically killed by his twin at the end of the play. It will be more difficult to think of an arc for characters who do not experience change, for example, Boxer in *Animal Farm*. BUT, you still need to think of their presentation at the beginning, middle and end of the text. Even if they don't change as a character, there is still something we can learn from them. It is shocking when Boxer is sent to the slaughterhouse despite his unwavering loyalty and hard work! Sometimes, it's the fact that the character remains stable and consistent when everyone around them is changing which is most interesting.

If you're quite confident about memorising quotations, you can take it up a level and start EMBEDDING one or two shorter quotations into your paragraphs. Examiners like embedded quotations. These shorter quotations don't need to be analysed, but you just throw them into your explanations so they naturally flow in the sentence, like this:

> At the beginning of 'An Inspector Calls', Sheila is presented as a spoilt and immature character who has a lot to learn about herself and wider society. This is evident when she receives her engagement ring from Gerald, and asks her mother, 'Look – Mummy – isn't it a beauty?' Here, the rhetorical question conveys Sheila's excitement, almost as if she is in awe of this expensive gift. It is clear at this point in the play that Sheila is 'pleased with life' and values material things – just like her parents – unaware of the hardships of the people around her who cannot afford such luxuries. However, the fact that she still feels the need to confirm whether the ring is 'beautiful' or not with her mother reveals her need for reassurance. The imperative 'look' makes it seem as though she is desperate for attention, and by referring to her mother as 'Mummy', Priestley subtly reveals how childish and immature Sheila is, with little independence or belief in herself as a woman.

If you've been paying attention, you will realise I haven't added any CONTEXT to the end of this paragraph yet. I know we looked at analysing quotations in detail in Paper 1, so in this section, I want to focus on how to END paragraphs and EVALUATE in more detail.

A good evaluation should include three things:

1. Integrating relevant context
2. Exploring the writer's message/intentions
3. Engaging with the effect on the audience

When you end your analysis, you need to think about WHY? WHY is the writer presenting a character in a certain way? What are they REPRESENTING? What CONTEXTUAL FACTORS do they link to? What was SOCIETY like at the time? What MESSAGE is the writer trying to convey?

Let's look at some examples from An Inspector Calls:

- Sheila is immature and superficial at the beginning of the play but becomes strong and independent by the end. WHY?

> During the time the play was set, women were only just beginning to find a voice within the patriarchal system of Edwardian society. Priestley may be using Sheila as a microcosm, to represent the rise of the Suffrage movement. By showing how Sheila gains a voice and gains power in the play, perhaps Priestley was encouraging the young women in the audience to do the same. #feministicon

- Mr Birling is presented as a foolish and ignorant character who predicts lots of things incorrectly, which the audience know are wrong. They are encouraged to laugh at him. WHY?

> Mr Birling represents capitalism in the play. So, Priestley may be using Mr Birling to symbolise how flawed capitalism was as a political ideology. By making his audience mock and ridicule Mr Birling's views, Priestley aligns his audience with socialism and implores them to accept the new Labour government.

- Mrs Birling promotes traditional gender roles by teaching Sheila to respect Gerald's status as a busy man. WHY?

> Priestley exposes Mrs Birling as a hypocrite as she clearly does not adhere to the traditional gender roles she asks Sheila to follow. She tells her husband off and lacks sympathy for a pregnant Eva Smith. Priestley uses her character as a vehicle to expose how some women help to perpetuate patriarchy and contribute to the oppression of women.

Does that make sense?

Let's try this with another text...

Lord of the Flies is about a group of British school boys who are stranded on an uninhabited island. They gradually turn savage, as they become influenced by a desire for power.

- The children begin as innocent and unable to commit violent acts. Gradually, they turn violent. WHY?

> Golding is drawing from his experience in World War Two, as well as the Cold War, to explore how even the most innocent people are capable of inherent savagery when influenced by the wider environment.

- Simon is a thoughtful, reflective and peaceful character who is viciously killed by the other boys. WHY?

> Perhaps Simon represents the religious and moral compass in the novel, and is even an allusion to Jesus, due to his rejection of violence and the brutal death he suffers because of his status as an outsider.

- The boys decide early on that only the individual with the conch is allowed to speak. WHY?

> Golding uses the conch as a symbol of civilisation and democracy. When the conch smashes later in the novel, it symbolises the boys' descent into barbarism and destruction.

Got it?

So, your overall essay will look something like this:

| 0 | 2 | How does Priestley present Sheila as a character who matures over the course of the play? |

Point

Introduces scene

Juicy quotation

Embedded quotation

Analysis

Context/ writer's message

Embedded quotation

At the beginning of 'An Inspector Calls', Sheila is presented as a spoilt and immature character who has a lot to learn about herself and wider society. This is evident when she receives her engagement ring from Gerald, and asks her mother, 'Look – Mummy – isn't it a beauty?' Here, the rhetorical question conveys Sheila's excitement, almost as if she is in awe of this expensive gift. It is clear at this point in the play that Sheila is 'pleased with life' and values material things – just like her parents – unaware of the hardships of the people around her who cannot afford such luxuries. However, the fact that she still feels the need to confirm whether the ring is 'beautiful' or not with her mother reveals her need for reassurance. The imperative 'look' makes it seem as though she is desperate for attention, and by having her refer to her mother as 'Mummy', Priestley subtly reveals how childish and immature Sheila is, with little independence or belief in herself as a woman. During the Edwardian era, women were expected to adhere to traditional gender roles, and through Sheila having these values imposed onto her by her mother, who teaches her that 'men who have important work to do' have a higher status than women, Priestley implies young women were being infantilised during this era and not seen as individuals in their own right.

Point

Introduces scene

Juicy quotation

Analysis

Embedded quotation

Context/ writer's message

However, as the play progresses, Sheila begins to feel empathy for the working class and challenges her parents' views, showing her growth in maturity. When Sheila learns about the part her father had to play in Eva's death, she exclaims, 'But these girls aren't cheap labour – they're people!' Here, the conjunction 'but' demonstrates how Sheila is beginning to disagree with her parents and is refusing to accept their treatment of the working class. Priestley's use of the exclamation mark in Sheila's speech symbolises how deeply remorseful she is about the way Eva was treated by her family. There is a clear juxtaposition between Sheila and her father in particular at this point, as she is the first member of the Birling family who acknowledges, and truly understands, the Inspector's message that 'we are members of one body.' During the Edwardian era, there was a significant class divide where the poor was exploited by the rich; the working class was stereotyped as lazy, and sometimes criminal too, and this allowed the rich people to justify their mistreatment of them. Hence, perhaps Priestley was using the character of Sheila as a vehicle to show the audience that the younger generation have the potential to challenge class inequality and, therefore, there is a hope for the future.

Point

Introduces scene

Juicy quotation

Analysis

Embedded quotation

Context/ writer's message

By the end of the play, Sheila matures into a young woman who has learnt the important lesson of accepting responsibility. After the Inspector leaves, she reminds her parents about the 'fire and blood and anguish' and says that 'it frightens me the way you talk.' Here, Sheila repeats the Inspector's words, cementing how she has entirely usurped his role and his beliefs. The use of polysyndeton displays Sheila's passion towards social responsibility, and also creates a sense of fluidity and strength within her speech, which contrasts to her earlier fragmented dialogue. By repeatedly using direct address, Sheila creates an accusatory tone, as if she is explicitly blaming her family for their discriminative actions. The fact that she now speaks using metaphors shows a progression from the 'silly girl' she was at the beginning of the play; the maturity in her language is emblematic of the maturity in her character. During the time the play was set, women were only just beginning to find a voice within the patriarchal system of Edwardian society. Therefore, Priestley may have been using Sheila as a microcosm, to represent the rise in the Suffrage movement. By showing how Sheila gains a voice and gains power in the play, perhaps Priestley was encouraging the young women in the audience to do the same.

That's a great essay, if I may say so myself.

For a theme or setting question, you could do the same thing and memorise THREE key quotations for the main themes if you wanted to, but if that seems like too much, you could just apply the appropriate character quotations you have already memorised to a theme.

For example, for a question about selfishness, I would use the quotations I already know about Mr Birling, Eva Smith (yes, she can come up even though she's dead) and Sheila.

These could be the key points:

- Paragraph 1: Priestley presents the selfishness of the rich through Mr Birling: 'a man has to ... look after himself – and his family too, of course, when he has one.'
- Paragraph 2: Priestley presents how selfishness can have detrimental consequences, using the death of Eva Smith: '... after swallowing disinfectant. Burnt her inside out, of course.'
- Paragraph 3: Sheila transforms from a selfish character to an empathetic one: 'fire and blood and anguish...'.

Simples.

Before moving on to the next section, why not pick one of your texts, write out a list of all the characters, and start selecting your THREE JUICIEST quotations for them (one from the BEGINNING, one from the MIDDLE, one from the END).

When you're ready...
let's move on to poetry!

TOP TIP!

When you're practising writing your own essay (maybe on how Mr Birling is presented?), you should have my Sheila essay open in front of you and try to use some of the same sentence starters to help you.

TOP TIP!

This method can help you revise your Shakespeare and 19th-century texts too!

Section B – POETRY (The ANTHOLOGY Question)

I'm going to start this section by writing you a poem, to get you in the poetry mood:

Roses are red,
Violets are blue,
GCSEs are tough,
But so are you.

Did you love it? Good.

Now, let's get on with it...

You will study 15 poems from the AQA Poetry Anthology in class – from the 'Love and Relationships' cluster, 'Power and Conflict' cluster or 'Worlds and Lives' cluster. This section of Paper 2 is where you will write an essay COMPARING two of those poems.

Because you're writing about TWO poems, you should aim to write FOUR paragraphs (two about each poem) in about 45 minutes.

There is no choice of question for this section. One poem will be printed for you and you will CHOOSE a second poem from the same cluster to compare it to.

This is what a question will look like:

0	2	Compare how poets present the effects of war in 'War Photographer' and in **one** other poem from 'Power and Conflict'.
		[30 marks]

I feel like we're pretty confident in how to write analytical paragraphs by now, but in poetry, there are some specific STRUCTURAL devices you should also be looking at.

When you're writing about your poems, ask yourself the following questions:

- Is this a **long** or **short** poem?
- Is there a **rhyme scheme**? Is it consistent or broken? Are there **rhyming couplets**?
- Are the stanzas the same length? (A **stanza** is another word for **paragraph** in poetry.)
- Is there **caesura** (any punctuation mark in the middle of a line)?
- Is there **enjambment** (no punctuation mark at the end of the line, and the sentence just rolls over onto the next line)?
- Is there a **cyclical structure**?

> **TOP TIP!**
>
> Also think about the FORM of the poem. Is it a sonnet, a dramatic monologue, or a narrative poem? Or maybe it's written in free verse, with no fixed structure at all?

'on't need to analyse the effect of ALL of these things – you can just pick
'hem for each poem and mention the effect of it somewhere in your essay.

' you a secret. I have some basic effects that I always adapt and apply
that comes up.

Here are some examples:

- If the stanzas are all the same length, this could show something is very strict or controlled.

- If the stanzas are varying in length and there is no fixed structure in the poem, it could show chaos – or maybe someone's emotions just pouring out onto the page.

- Caesura creates a little pause in the line, so perhaps you could say this slows down the pace of the poem and shows time is passing slowly. OR maybe you could say it creates a break in the line, symbolising the person is broken…

- Enjambment speeds up the pace of the poem (because the sentence just runs onto the next line) and maybe this shows the speaker's frustration. OR maybe it creates a break in the sentence, showing two people will never be together…

That's good, isn't it? You're welcome. So, this is how you would bring some structure analysis into your paragraph:

> In the poem 'War Photographer', Duffy portrays the effect of war as distressing, not just for soldiers but for spectators too: 'spools of suffering set out in ordered rows.' Here, the use of the hyperbolic metaphor in 'spools of suffering' conveys how the photographer defines the images he has taken during his time in the war zone through pain and trauma. It's like the photographs are alive and still haunting him, and the use of the plural 'spools' emphasises the extent and magnitude of the suffering he witnessed. Yet it is only now that he is facing the victims behind the photographs for the first time; just like the photos are developing slowly, so is his memory, as he processes the events he endured. The sibilance creates a soft tone, which highlights his desire to escape the noise of war he left behind – as if he's feeling a sense of respite alone in his 'dark room'. Duffy's use of the verb 'set out' could perhaps symbolise coffins, suggesting death is constantly on the photographer's mind, and it also literally conveys his desperation to give order to something as chaotic as war. This sense of desperation to find salvation – but failure to do so – is reinforced structurally through the use of enjambment in the first two lines, which mirrors how his trauma cannot be regulated or controlled – it simply spills out. Thus, Duffy seems to be concerned about the lasting impact of bottling up emotions in war and is particularly interested in the psychological impact of war. Even though the photographer is far away physically, he cannot detach from what he observed.

Annotations:
- Point that answers the question, using words from the question
- Juicy quotation
- Embedded quotation
- Language analysis (starting with basic and becoming more perceptive)
- Reinforces point with structure
- Links to context/ poet's message

See how it just flows in after my language analysis to reinforce my point?

So, that's structure done. ✓

The other main difference in this exam is the fact that you are COMPARING two poems, and that's the bit that really gets students…

So, how do you compare?

Well, think about these two pictures:

The first picture is of roses and the second is of poppies.

COMPARE means looking at BOTH similarities AND differences, so let's begin by thinking, what is the link between the images? Well, they are both flowers. Duh. They are both part of the natural world.

That link is how you begin your essay:

> Both 'Roses' and 'Poppies' are flowers and a part of the natural world.

Next, let's follow our paragraph structure for the first picture only:

> Both 'Roses' and 'Poppies' are flowers and a part of the natural world. In 'Roses', Baig presents the natural world as beautiful: 'Juicy quotation'. Analyse. Evaluate.

Next, you add a COMPARATIVE CONNECTIVE ('Similarly', 'However', 'On the other hand', etc) and follow the same paragraph structure for the second picture:

> Both 'Roses' and 'Poppies' are flowers and a part of the natural world. In 'Roses', Baig presents the natural world as beautiful: 'Juicy quotation'. Analyse. Evaluate.
> Similarly, in 'Poppies', Baigel also presents the natural world as picturesque: 'Juicy quotation'. Analyse. Evaluate.

NOW... this is the important bit...

At the end of this second paragraph is where you really go in with your comparison, thinking about WHY those similarities or differences exist. Even though roses and poppies are both beautiful, they are different because roses are used more in romantic relationships, and poppies are used in remembrance of soldiers who died in war. So WHY did the poets choose to present these different flowers? What message were they trying to give?

> Both 'Roses' and 'Poppies' are flowers and a part of the natural world. In 'Roses', Baig presents the natural world as beautiful: 'Juicy quotation'. Analyse. Evaluate.
>
> **Comparative connective**
> Similarly, in 'Poppies', Baigel also presents the natural world as picturesque: 'Juicy quotation'. Analyse. Evaluate. Although 'Roses' and 'Poppies' are similar in the way they add beauty to their surroundings, they are different because roses are used to enhance the romantic relationship between lovers, whereas poppies are used to **Comparative conclusion** beautify the dead soldiers, to show how there was a greater purpose and glory behind their sacrifice. Hence, perhaps Baig wanted to demonstrate the beauty found in life, whereas Baigel was more concerned with how beauty can still be found even in the most unlikely places, like death.

That's two paragraphs done. And then you would repeat the same thing again for your next two paragraphs.

Shall we apply what we've learnt to our exam question?

0 2	Compare how poets present the effects of war in 'War Photographer' and in **one** other poem from 'Power and Conflict'.

[30 marks]

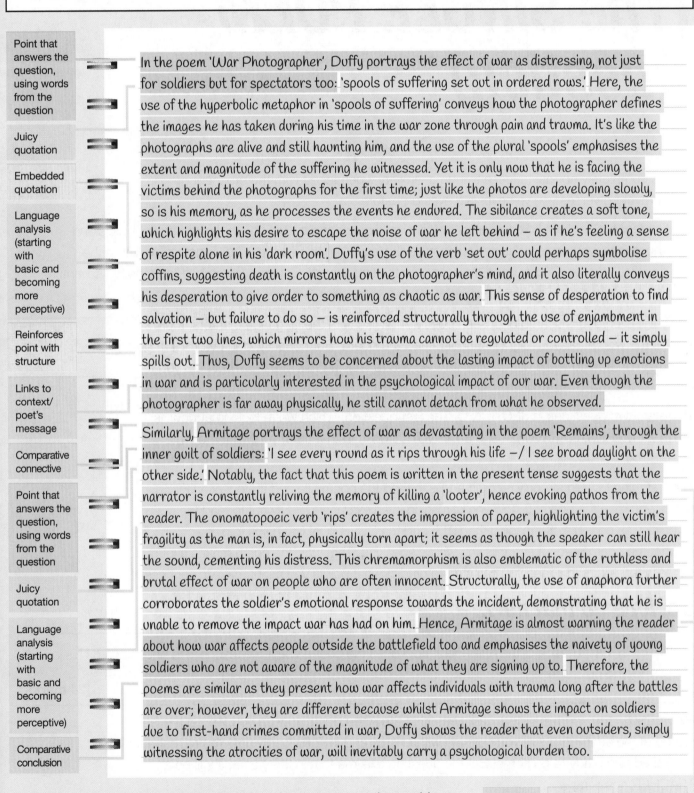

Point that answers the question, using words from the question

Juicy quotation

Embedded quotation

Language analysis (starting with basic and becoming more perceptive)

Reinforces point with structure

Links to context/ poet's message

Comparative connective

Point that answers the question, using words from the question

Juicy quotation

Language analysis (starting with basic and becoming more perceptive)

Comparative conclusion

In the poem 'War Photographer', Duffy portrays the effect of war as distressing, not just for soldiers but for spectators too: 'spools of suffering set out in ordered rows.' Here, the use of the hyperbolic metaphor in 'spools of suffering' conveys how the photographer defines the images he has taken during his time in the war zone through pain and trauma. It's like the photographs are alive and still haunting him, and the use of the plural 'spools' emphasises the extent and magnitude of the suffering he witnessed. Yet it is only now that he is facing the victims behind the photographs for the first time; just like the photos are developing slowly, so is his memory, as he processes the events he endured. The sibilance creates a soft tone, which highlights his desire to escape the noise of war he left behind – as if he's feeling a sense of respite alone in his 'dark room'. Duffy's use of the verb 'set out' could perhaps symbolise coffins, suggesting death is constantly on the photographer's mind, and it also literally conveys his desperation to give order to something as chaotic as war. This sense of desperation to find salvation – but failure to do so – is reinforced structurally through the use of enjambment in the first two lines, which mirrors how his trauma cannot be regulated or controlled – it simply spills out. Thus, Duffy seems to be concerned about the lasting impact of bottling up emotions in war and is particularly interested in the psychological impact of our war. Even though the photographer is far away physically, he still cannot detach from what he observed.

Similarly, Armitage portrays the effect of war as devastating in the poem 'Remains', through the inner guilt of soldiers: 'I see every round as it rips through his life –/ I see broad daylight on the other side.' Notably, the fact that this poem is written in the present tense suggests that the narrator is constantly reliving the memory of killing a 'looter', hence evoking pathos from the reader. The onomatopoeic verb 'rips' creates the impression of paper, highlighting the victim's fragility as the man is, in fact, physically torn apart; it seems as though the speaker can still hear the sound, cementing his distress. This chremamorphism is also emblematic of the ruthless and brutal effect of war on people who are often innocent. Structurally, the use of anaphora further corroborates the soldier's emotional response towards the incident, demonstrating that he is unable to remove the impact war has had on him. Hence, Armitage is almost warning the reader about how war affects people outside the battlefield too and emphasises the naivety of young soldiers who are not aware of the magnitude of what they are signing up to. Therefore, the poems are similar as they present how war affects individuals with trauma long after the battles are over; however, they are different because whilst Armitage shows the impact on soldiers due to first-hand crimes committed in war, Duffy shows the reader that even outsiders, simply witnessing the atrocities of war, will inevitably carry a psychological burden too.

Use this template and try writing about how love, power, or the world we live in is presented in two other poems of your choice... you'll feel a lot better once you've given it a go yourself, I promise.

Links to context/ poet's message

Reinforces point with structure

Embedded quotation

And then, let's move on to the next section!

Section C – UNSEEN POETRY (The SINGLE POEM Question)

For more on this, see my video:

Welcome, brave GCSE students, to the intriguing world of unseen poetry!

It's completely normal to feel a twinge of anxiety when faced with the prospect of unravelling verses you've never laid eyes on before.

But fear not, for I am here to demystify this poetic quest and assure you that, with the right tools and knowledge, you can cast aside your worries like leaves in the autumn wind. Together, we'll turn the daunting into the delightful and the scary into the sensational. Get ready to embark on a poetic adventure.

Basically, everyone is scared of unseen poetry. A bit like with the language extracts, there's always the worry that you might not understand the poem. But honestly, don't worry. I'm going to teach you how to feel more confident when you're tackling this question and help you to write a TOP LEVEL essay on it!

There are two questions in SECTION C. The first question, which we're looking at now, is worth 24 MARKS, so you will spend 30 MINUTES on it. In that time, you will try to write THREE PARAGRAPHS.

The first thing I would strongly recommend is to read the poem title and the question FIRST, before you read the poem. I know you're rushing in an exam, and you want to read the poem as quickly as possible, but reading the TITLE and the QUESTION first helps to give you an idea of what the poem is about and tells you who is speaking. That way, the poem makes a lot more sense when you read it, and you can start to predict what points you might make in your essay.

So, let's do that now:

> | 0 | 1 | In 'Last Lesson of the Afternoon', how does the poet present the teacher's feelings towards his job and his students?
>
> **[24 marks]**

Right… so… the poem is called 'Last Lesson of the Afternoon'. How do you feel on the last lesson of the afternoon? Are you bursting with energy and joy? Probably not. You're probably quite tired and ready to go home. But the question tells me that in this poem, it will be a TEACHER speaking.

How do you think teachers feel on the last lesson of the afternoon? I'm guessing the same. UNLESS this poem is about a teacher who really LOVES his job and LOVES the LAST LESSON OF THE DAY. I doubt it… but let's read the poem and find out.

Last Lesson of the Afternoon

When will the bell ring, and end this weariness?
How long have they tugged the leash, and strained apart,
My pack of unruly hounds! I cannot start
Them again on a quarry of knowledge they hate to hunt,
5   I can haul them and urge them no more.

No longer now can I endure the brunt
Of the books that lie out on the desks; a full threescore
Of several insults of blotted pages, and scrawl
Of slovenly work that they have offered me.
10   I am sick, and what on earth is the good of it all?
What good to them or me, I cannot see!

                                        So, shall I take
My last dear fuel of life to heap on my soul
And kindle my will to a flame that shall consume
15   Their dross of indifference; and take the toll
Of their insults in punishment? — I will not! —

I will not waste my soul and my strength for this.
What do I care for all that they do amiss!
What is the point of this teaching of mine, and of this
20   Learning of theirs? It all goes down the same abyss.

What does it matter to me, if they can write
A description of a dog, or if they can't?
What is the point? To us both, it is all my aunt!
And yet I'm supposed to care, with all my might.

25   I do not, and will not; they won't and they don't; and that's all!
I shall keep my strength for myself; they can keep theirs as well.
Why should we beat our heads against the wall
Of each other? I shall sit and wait for the bell.

D.H. Lawrence

Right… it's safe to say this teacher does not love his job very much. He seems bored, frustrated and exhausted. Those are going to be my three points.

So now what?

It is human nature to look at this poem and focus on all the words you don't understand, so you might be sitting in your exam, sweating and shaking, looking at *'quarry'*, *'slovenly'*, and *'dross of indifference'* and think… I can't do this.

And at that point, I want you to take a deep breath, and I want you to remember my wise words:

Don't worry about what you don't know!
Focus on what you DO know!

The examiner will NEVER KNOW about the words you didn't understand. All you need to do, is pick out THREE quotations you DO understand. As always, try to look for JUICY QUOTATIONS… quotations with lots of interesting words and language devices in them.

In this poem, I really like the following quotations:

1 *'When will the bell ring, and end this weariness?'*
2 *'My pack of unruly hounds!'*
3 *'I will not waste my soul and my strength for this.'*

Once I've got my quotations, I can start analysing. Remember all the things I've taught you so far… Because your MARKS LIE IN YOUR ANALYSIS, the more interesting things you can say about the quotation, the higher the mark you will get.

Really stare at the quotation to see what language devices are hiding in there. Start off with the basic explanation, then work your way up to more original and perceptive interpretations.

- What will **ALL** the class say about this quotation?
- What will **HALF** the class say about this quotation?
- What can **ONLY YOU** say about this quotation?

1 *'When will the bell ring, and end this weariness?'*
- Rhetorical question – teacher is questioning why he is doing this job. Doesn't understand the purpose anymore.
- 'Ring' is onomatopoeic – he is fantasising about the sound of the bell.
- Alliteration 'w' – creates a quivering effect, like the job is causing him distress/physical fatigue.

2 *'My pack of unruly hounds!'*
- Metaphor 'hounds' – students are wild, uncontrollable.
- Exclamation mark – anger, desperately trying to control them.
- Zoomorphism – makes them seem dangerous; teacher is frightened.
- Collective noun 'pack' – he is outnumbered.
- Possessive pronoun 'my' – he still feels responsible for his students.

3 *'I will not waste my soul and my strength for this.'*
- Sibilance – soft sound: he is tired and running out of energy.
- Declarative sentence 'I will not' – he has given up and will not change his mind.
- Religious imagery 'soul' – he is almost praying for God to save him.

Perfect! We're getting there.

But don't forget… we need to add STRUCTURE. Now, I asked myself all the structure questions…

- Is this a long or short poem?
- Is there a rhyme scheme? Is it consistent or broken? Are there rhyming couplets?
- Are the stanzas the same length?
- Is there caesura?
- Is there enjambment?
- Is there a cyclical structure?

… and I noticed something really clever…

Did you spot it?

This poem has a CYCLICAL structure – the first line mentions 'the bell' and so does the last line! So, I'm definitely going to talk about that. I also might mention the fact that it's quite a long poem – what could that symbolise? Or the fact that there is no rhyme scheme.

Shall we put all of that together?

Here's a full Unseen Poetry essay on this question:

> | 0 | 1 | In 'Last Lesson of the Afternoon', how does the poet present the teacher's feelings towards his job and his students?
>
> **[24 marks]**

Firstly, in 'Last Lesson of the Afternoon', Lawrence presents the teacher's feelings of boredom towards his job: 'When will the bell ring, and end this weariness?' Here, the rhetorical question creates the impression that the teacher is questioning why he is doing this job, as if he doesn't understand the purpose of it anymore. 'Ring' is onomatopoeic, and it seems as though the teacher is fantasising about the end of the lesson, as if the mere sound of the bell could bring the teacher a semblance of relief. The alliteration of 'w' creates a quivering effect, accentuating the distress the teacher feels due to the challenges he faces at work. This idea is further reinforced by Lawrence's use of the cyclical structure, which is emblematic of how trapped the teacher feels within this profession; the repeated reference to the 'bell' at the beginning and the end of the poem cements his desperate yearning for release from the monotony of his job.

Moreover, as the poem progresses, the teacher's frustration towards his job and students becomes more evident: 'My pack of unruly hounds!' Lawrence's use of the metaphor 'hounds' makes the students seem wild and uncontrollable, highlighting their bad behaviour. The exclamation mark emphasises the teacher's anger towards their disobedience, and creates the impression he is raising his voice as he desperately tries to control them. This zoomorphism makes the students almost seem savage and dangerous, and suggests the teacher is frightened of them. This idea is further corroborated through the collective noun 'pack'; the teacher is clearly outnumbered by his students and seems vulnerable. However, the possessive pronoun 'my' subtly reveals that the teacher still cares about his students, despite their rebellion, as he feels a sense of responsibility towards them. Perhaps this is why he is even more disappointed and frustrated by their poor behaviour and 'slovenly work' – because he realises that their failure as students is indicative of his failure as a teacher.

Annotations (right margin):

- Point that answers the question, using words from the question
- Juicy quotation
- Refers back to the question
- Language analysis (starting with basic and becoming more perceptive)
- Point that answers the question, using words from the question
- Reinforces point with structure
- Juicy quotation
- Analyses punctuation
- Refers back to the question
- Embedded quotation

Furthermore, the poet presents how the teacher's job and students have left him feeling exhausted: 'I will not waste my soul and my strength for this.' Here, the sibilance creates a soft sound, and this is emblematic of how tired the teacher is, as if he is running out of energy. The declarative sentence 'I will not' portrays how he has given up on his job and his students and will not change his mind. Lawrence creates a real sense of the teacher's distress through the religious imagery 'soul'; it is almost as if he is praying for God to save him. The teacher has reached a point of surrender, and is unwilling to invest any more of himself into a profession that has drained him. The verb 'waste' further encapsulates his deep dissatisfaction with his job, as he sees no value in it anymore, and it also implies a sense of emotional and physical fatigue – and this is reinforced through the long length of the poem. Perhaps Lawrence was using this poem to convey the complex and tumultuous feelings of the teacher, shedding light on his profound disillusionment with both his job and his students. The message of the poem seems to be to highlight the universal struggles of those in the teaching profession, clearly showing the reader the toll that such a demanding profession can take on the human spirit.

Point that answers the question, using words from the question

Juicy quotation

Language analysis (starting with basic and becoming more perceptive)

Reinforces point with structure

Summarises the message of the poem

So, to summarise ALL of that, these are the steps you need to follow to tackle the first question of Unseen Poetry:

- Read the question and the title before you read the poem! This will help you to understand the poem, and who is speaking.
- Ignore the bits you don't understand.
- Focus on THREE QUOTATIONS you do understand.
- Try to make sure the quotations you choose are JUICY – identify language devices.
- Write down ALL the things you can get from one quotation.
- Add how this is reinforced through the structure or form.
- Link to the poet's message.

And will the examiner ever know we didn't know what *'quarry'* meant? No!

Section C – UNSEEN POETRY (The COMPARISON Question)

Don't worry about this bit too much. It's a little baby question – it's only 8 marks. Of course, we will try our best as always, but I don't want you stressing out too much about it. You will spend no more than 15 minutes on this question and write two paragraphs only. AQA will give you another unseen poem and ask you to compare the two unseen poems.

The key thing to remember in this question is that you are comparing the METHODS used in both unseen poems, and thinking about WHY different techniques have been used. Try to cover both language and structure, and show off as much (relevant) subject terminology as possible.

Don't worry if you're confused – just look at this.

Here is a second unseen poem that we will be comparing to 'Last Lesson of the Afternoon':

Your Dad Did What?

Where they have been, if they have been away,
or what they've done at home, if they have not –
you make them write about the holiday.
One writes My Dad did. What? Your Dad did what?

5 That's not a sentence. Never mind the bell.
We stay behind until the work is done.
You count their words (you who can count and spell);
all the assignments are complete bar one

and though this boy seems bright, that one is his.
10 He says he's finished, doesn't want to add
anything, hands it in just as it is.
No change. My Dad did. What? What did his Dad?

You find the 'E' you gave him as you sort
through reams of what this girl did, what that lad did,
15 and read the line again, just one 'e' short:
This holiday was horrible. My Dad did.

Sophie Hannah

0 2 In both 'Last Lesson of the Afternoon' and 'Your Dad Did What?' the poets describe ideas about the teachers' strong emotions.
What are the similarities **and/or** differences between the methods the poets use to present these ideas?

[8 marks]

I love this poem – I think it's so sad. Read it again if you're not sure what it's about… there's a twist at the end.

Let me give you a minute to figure it out…

Do you get it?

His dad died during the holidays… that's why he didn't want to write about it. But the teacher – overworked and tired and stressed – kept telling him off because she couldn't figure out what he was trying to say.

Now, because they want you to focus on METHODS in this question, let's think: what language devices are used in both 'Last Lesson of the Afternoon' and 'Your Dad Did What?'.

Well, I can see that both poems use QUESTIONS. THAT is my first sentence:

Both 'Your Dad Did What?' and 'Last Lesson of the Afternoon' use questions to convey the teachers' strong emotions.

Next, we will explain WHY each poet uses questions, and the effect of them. In 'Last Lesson of the Afternoon', the teacher isn't asking anyone the questions, is he? He's kind of just asking himself to show how pointless he thinks his job is. But in 'Your Dad Did What?', the teacher is repeatedly asking the student questions, because she is so frustrated with the boy. Let's write that out:

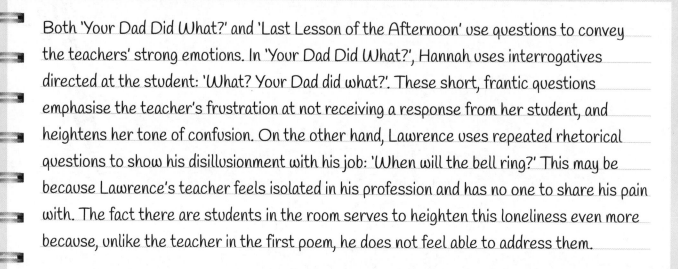

Both 'Your Dad Did What?' and 'Last Lesson of the Afternoon' use questions to convey the teachers' strong emotions. In 'Your Dad Did What?', Hannah uses interrogatives directed at the student: 'What? Your Dad did what?'. These short, frantic questions emphasise the teacher's frustration at not receiving a response from her student, and heightens her tone of confusion. On the other hand, Lawrence uses repeated rhetorical questions to show his disillusionment with his job: 'When will the bell ring?' This may be because Lawrence's teacher feels isolated in his profession and has no one to share his pain with. The fact there are students in the room serves to heighten this loneliness even more because, unlike the teacher in the first poem, he does not feel able to address them.

And then we do the same thing with another METHOD comparison. I will talk about a difference now, just because I think I've found a good one. (I could do two similarities if I wanted to.) In 'Last Lesson of the Afternoon', Lawrence uses first person – *'I shall sit and wait for the bell'* – because it's all about HIS feelings and emotions… but in 'Your Dad Did What?', Hannah uses second person – *'YOU who can count and spell'* – because she is judging the teacher's mistake.

However, the poems use narrative perspective differently. Hannah employs the second person, 'you who can count and spell', which creates an accusatory tone as if the narrator is blaming the teacher for her lack of empathy. On the other hand, Lawrence uses a first-person perspective: 'I shall sit and wait for the bell'. This elicits empathy for him as readers can understand his conflict as he feels trapped in a job he does not enjoy anymore. The differing perspectives allow both poets to convey different levels of empathy for the teachers.

Done. That's it. That's everything.

OMG… we have actually covered everything. That is wild.

I am so proud of you for getting through this guide, honestly.

Now go and have a lovely warm bath… go for a long walk… drink lots of water… and have a well-deserved break.

I'm going to leave you with a parting poem that I wrote especially for you:

Roses are red,
Violets are blue,
Believe in yourself,
As I believe in you.

Final Thoughts from Mehreen

There are a few things I always suggest my students do during the lead-up to the exams, and I want to share them with you now. If you have the time, try to start these good habits at least a couple of weeks before your exams begin, so that your body can get used to the new routine and start feeling the benefits.

Start waking up early at least two weeks before the exams begin, so your body clock gets used to it. That way, you won't be too tired on the morning of the GCSEs. I do this even now – if I have a big job coming up that I know I have to wake up really early for, I start waking up at that time two weeks in advance, so that I'm fresh on the day.

Start going for long walks (at least half an hour) preferably in a park or an area with greenery, every day. This could be early in the morning, so you're feeling awake and alert, and your mind is clear to the tackle the day… or it could be in the evening, to clear your mind before you sleep (I do both!). Daily walks are great to help with nerves and anxiety.

You want to be hydrated and glowing for the exams, so start drinking water and eating healthily in advance too. The more water and nutrients you feed your body, the better your body and mind will feel. And you need to feel good to perform at your best.

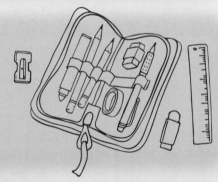

You do NOT want to be stressing out, flustered and flapping around on the morning of the exam. So, make sure you get everything organised the night before. Have your uniform laid out – and I mean shoes, socks, everything – and have your pencil case ready too. On the morning of the exam, all you want to worry about is showering, getting dressed and having a filling, healthy breakfast (like porridge or eggs).

Get to school nice and early on the morning of the exam, so you're as relaxed as possible and have time to look over any revision notes.

People often think GCSEs are the end… but they're not. They're the beginning. These exams are the beginning of the rest of your life. Whether they go to plan or not, you will learn from this experience, and use those lessons to move forward in life. ALL you can do is try your best. That is literally all you can do.

So, go out there and show them what you're made of.

Mehreen

xxx

Search 'Glow Up Your Grades' online to find more of my videos to help with your revision.

ACKNOWLEDGEMENTS

The author and publisher are grateful to the copyright holders for permission to use quoted materials and images.

Pages 4, 5, 11, 12, 85, 86, 88, 89 quotes from 'An Inspector Calls' by J. B. Priestley (plays first published by William Heinemann 1948-50, first published by Penguin Books 1969, Penguin Classics 2000). 'An Inspector Calls' copyright 1947 by J. B. Priestley; Page 7 'Winter Swans' by Owen Sheers ©Owen Sheers; Page 8 'Mother, any distance' by Simon Armitage ©Simon Armitage, used with permission; Page 33 extract by Hannah de Leuw; Page 91, 93 'War Photographer' by Carol Ann Duffy ©Carol Ann Duffy; Page 93 'Remains' by Simon Armitage ©Simon Armitage, used with permission; Page 99, 100 'Your Dad Did What?' from 'Marrying the Ugly Millionaire: New and Collected Poems' by Sophie Hannah.

The author would like to thank Lulu Azapovic-Sasaoka for her editorial contribution.

Every effort has been made to trace copyright holders and obtain their permission for the use of copyright material. The author and publisher will gladly receive information enabling them to rectify any error or omission in subsequent editions.

All facts are correct at time of going to press.

All images ©Shutterstock and HarperCollinsPublishers

Published by Collins
An imprint of HarperCollinsPublishers Limited
1 London Bridge Street, London SE1 9GF

HarperCollinsPublishers
Macken House, 39/40 Mayor Street Upper
Dublin 1, D01 C9W8, Ireland

Contribution © Mehreen Baig 2024

ISBN 978-0-00-866497-8
First published 2024
10 9 8 7 6 5 4 3 2 1

British Library Cataloguing in Publication Data.

A CIP record of this book is available from the British Library.

Publisher: Katie Sergeant
Author: Mehreen Baig
Project Manager: Katie Galloway
Copyeditor and Proofreader: Marian Olney
Internal Concept Design: Ian Wrigley
Photographs: James Rudland Photography
Layout: Rose & Thorn Creative Services Ltd
Cover Design: Sarah Duxbury and Amparo Barrera
Production: Bethany Brohm
Printed in the United Kingdom by Martins the Printers

FSC™ C007454
MIX
Paper | Supporting responsible forestry
www.fsc.org

This book contains FSC™ certified paper and other controlled sources to ensure responsible forest management.

For more information visit: www.harpercollins.co.uk/green